Building a

Revelation

Superhighway

By Hearing, Seeing, and Perceiving in the Spirit

Sarah,
you are a treasure! I am
so blessed to know you & I
look forward to how He will
weave our stories together!

Kathleen Schmeuszer

Kathy

ISBN: 978-1-60383-446-9

Published by:
Holy Fire Publishing
PO Box 540693
Merritt Island, FL 32954

www.ChristianPublish.com

Printed in the United States of America and the United Kingdom

Dedication

I would like to dedicate this book to The Lord. This is a step of obedience and an expression of my love for Him and His for me.

I want to thank my wonderful husband and daughter, Doug and Kristina, who supported me while I wrote, emotionally, spiritually and practically. You are the best! I also want to dedicate this book to my two wonderful grown sons, Michael and Andrew. I am so proud of both of you. I am blessed to be your mom!

I also want to say a hearty "Thank you!" filled with more love and appreciation than you could know to my editors and friends: Gracie, Francine, Zelma, Georgette, and Mary.

Thank you also to all of the contributors to the testimony section. You are wonderful living examples of allowing heaven and earth to connect in you from your intimate communion with Him. I thank God for you all.

Table of Contents

Introduction

The whole earth is groaning for the revealing of the sons of God. How will these sons be revealed to the earth unless the sons receive the revelation of who they are first? How can the sons have revelation of who they are without the Spirit revealing also who He is? How can we live, move, and possess our being in the Spirit without divine revelation? We cannot. We **must** hear God. We must increase our capacity to receive from Him. That is the purpose of this book. This course is designed to be experiential in nature. The vast majority of what you receive from this book and the workbook will come from God alone as you do the exercises and homework with Him. The purpose is not just to give you information but also to lead you to receiving divine revelation directly from the Lord. The information contained in this course is designed to give you a place to start in receiving revelation in an increased measure, to give you encouragement, and to provide some helpful guidelines along the way.

I had a word from the Lord a couple of years ago. In part of the word He said very strongly, "Build Me a trench!" What He showed me with these words was a structure in the form of a trench with water flowing through it from heaven into me and out through me to the world. I knew the "trench" was an open channel of communication and power. The trench was depicted to me by the Lord as a wooden structure with water flowing, as a highway through a wilderness, and also as a gangway connecting two places. We are the trench. We are to be the gangway. The Highway of Heaven is built in us. Just as angels were seen ascending and descending on Jacob's ladder, we are to have activity of the spirit realm going back and forth in us, like a multi-lane highway with traffic flowing in both directions. Prayer goes up, and revelation and power come down. In fact, since we are seated with Him in heavenly places, we are up. The Holy Spirit is also indwelling us on earth. We are, according to the Word, in two places at once.

This is why I have entitled this book *Building a Revelation Superhighway*. We do this by hearing, seeing, and perceiving in the Spirit. Heaven meets earth in us. Eternity meets mortality in us. The unseen realm meets the seen. We are the portals of heaven on the earth. Let us be open vessels that receive revelation and power from heaven and pour it out on the world around us.

So then dear reader, I speak over you now in the blessed Name of Jesus Christ. I speak to your capacity to see and know and understand in the Spirit and say "Be increased!" I agree with God over you that, as His disciple, your ears are blessed and can hear Him clearly. I agree with God over you that your eyes can see! I agree that your understanding, imagination, and mental capabilities are enlightened and are being increasingly made to see. I agree with God that the results of this increased ability to receive revelation from Him will result in your knowing without a doubt what the hope of His calling is. You will also know in increasing measure what are the riches of His inheritance in the saints and what is the exceeding greatness of His power toward us and in us who believe. Amen!

My desire is to remove any road blocks in our thinking that keep us from this open communion with God. The main thought we need to destroy is this: "I must be spiritual enough or reach a certain spiritual level to hear God the way I want to hear Him." The good news of the gospel is that we are clean and righteous before God through the blood of Jesus Christ. There is no other level to be obtained. There is nothing else to strive for. We have access through The Blood to come boldly into His Presence. Let this good news of the gospel sink deep into your heart and mind and set you free to live, move, and have your being in the Spirit!

As spiritual beings living and moving in the Spirit, we need the revelation of God. We need the words of God. We need our minds enlightened to see and know and fully grasp all He has provided for us in Jesus Christ. As we have many streams or lanes of revelation flowing to and through us, we will realize our true nature as the sons of God. We will be open "gates" or portals of heaven that He can flow through. He wants to build a supernatural superhighway right through you!

Chapter 1

Blessed Are My Ears, They Hear!

This section of the book will begin with two understood and accepted premises. The first is that God wants to have a relationship with you so much that He gave His only Son to restore you to Himself. The second is that, as a born again believer, you have all the ability you need to come and talk with Him and hear His voice because of the Blood of Christ. There is no effort or goodness on your part that would make you acceptable or any lack that would make you unacceptable. It is only being a recipient of His shed Blood that enables us to stand in His presence. There is nothing that needs to be added to it, and nothing that we do can take away from it or diminish its power to make us righteous before Him. When you believe this, there is nothing to hinder your fellowship together!

Relationship involves communication. You really can't have a relationship without it. Even long distance relationships have letters and, these days, e-mail and Skype. In Scripture, God reveals Himself as Father, mother hen, brother, friend, and spouse. He is wooing us, seeking our affections and hearts. He is drawing us with word pictures of our closest relationships. He is using these words to let us know the kind of close relationship He desires to have with us. He wants to communicate with us.

We have the Scriptures to bring us to Him. They show us what He is like and all that He has done for us in sending Jesus to be Emmanuel, God with us. The Bible even tells us what He says and what He thinks about us. I liken Scripture to a love poem from my Beloved. Picture a love poem being read by a woman from her lover who is away at war. It is one level of intimacy for her to read the poem and know he wrote it to her; it is another level of intimacy for her to sit face to face with him and experience him spontaneously speaking words of love to her. The words and the meaning may be the same in both scenarios, but the level of a poem's ability to melt her heart increases when she hears him say it. In this same way, we need to hear the Lord's voice speaking to us. Scripture is supposed to bring us to Him in a relationship that is face to face. Listen to what Jesus said to the religious people of His day.

> John 5:39-40 *"You search the Scriptures, for in them you think you have eternal life; and these are they which testify of Me, but you are not willing to come to Me that you may have life."*

Let that not be true of us. May we come to Him so that we might have life.

We are to live by His words.

Jesus says in Matthew 4:4 that we shouldn't live by bread alone, but that we should live from every word that proceeds from the mouth of God. Coming to Him and hearing words He speaks to us are what we are to LIVE by! That word "proceeds" is in a present continuous tense. Jesus is not saying we should live by what He said yesterday or years ago. He is saying we should live by or from the constant flow of words from His mouth. Jesus modeled this for us by saying and living out that He only said what He heard the Father saying and only did what He saw the Father doing. That is the definition of "living by His words".

When we live by His words we will bear fruit by them.

> John 15:7-8 *"If you abide in Me, and My words abide in you, you will ask what you desire, and it shall be done for you. By this My Father is glorified, that you bear much fruit; so you will be My disciples."*

Faith is increased by His words

When we live by His words we will also increase our faith by them. Romans 10:17 says, *"So then faith comes by hearing, and hearing by the word of God."* Hearing His words, His utterance, increases our faith. If we can hear God say it, we can believe it! This Scripture points out that your ability to hear is not in question, nor is your faith. Ultimately, the foundation of our faith and hearing rests securely, and without question, on the fact that He speaks to us. My paraphrase of the verse would go something like this: Faith comes by the act of hearing, and hearing comes because He is saying something.

The Spirit of God is speaking.

John 16:13-14 tells us:

> *"However when He, the Spirit of truth, has come, He will guide you into all truth; for He will not speak on His own authority, but whatever He hears He will speak, and He will tell you things to come. He will glorify Me, for He will take of what is Mine and declare it to you."*

When it seems He's not talking to me

Maybe you know that He is speaking and that you need these words to live by, but your experience with hearing Him has been rare or seemingly random. Maybe you have yet to be able to purposefully tune into the flow of words inside you that the Spirit is speaking. Sometimes this can build a wall in our hearts, where we believe the lie that He is talking to everyone but me. I would like to share a testimony with you from our family.

My husband and I were teachers in a discipleship program we started when we lived in Germany. We taught the students a course on hearing God. We taught what we knew then, including tips on how to quiet your mind to hear. We explained the many ways to hear from God. We had

Scriptures, examples, and testimonies. All three of our children sat in on every one of these classes. I assumed that they had no problem hearing God. I was wrong.

After we had moved back to the States, my daughter Kristina became frustrated with what she thought was God's silence toward her. Nothing I said, none of my information, helped her. She became angry and hurt. I was at a loss, so I just prayed for her. Then I remembered a book I had read of a missionary to India who would sit and listen to God with lost people about problems in their lives. When the lost person heard something they had to promise to do it. Without fail, obeying God solved their problems! They gave their hearts to God and turned from all other gods. One night, after talking with my daughter about her frustrations, I told her that I would spend time hearing God with her and helping her. A few days later, she came with me to a job I had that just involved sitting at an 'open house' as people came to see it. We sat in our lawn chairs on the front porch. She pulled out her Bible and two notebooks and said, "Now you can teach me to hear God." Outwardly I was very calm, but inwardly I was beseeching God to come through for my baby! Oh me of little faith! But thank God it only takes a little. I told her that I believed she was hearing God and asked her if she believed I could hear God. She said she did. I said we would ask God a question and I would listen and write down the answer. I told her to write down what she *thought she imagined* Jesus would say. It didn't have to be God, just what she supposed He would say if He were sitting in front of her. Then I told her that God's voice to her would sound like her thoughts and would come out the way she talked, and God's voice to me would sound more like I talk, so the answers would be the same answer, but not identical because of this. She understood. For our first question, we asked Him what He thought was her greatest strength. We got the same answer! By the second or third question, tears were streaming down her face! "All this time God was talking to me, and I thought it was just me!" She was overcome with joy. We sat on the porch and asked God questions together for five hours getting the same answers from Him. Once He told me that He was going to tell her something extra that I couldn't or wouldn't hear for myself. So I wrote that down. What an awesome confirmation as she hesitatingly said, "Oh and I've heard something else from God - off subject."

Somehow releasing my daughter to just write what she thought He was saying, and relieving her of the pressure of having to decide if it was really God, freed the flow of divine communication in her. She was able to hear unhindered by anxiety. I exhort you to do the exercises at the end of this chapter with the same freedom. You could pair up with someone and write what you *imagine* He *may* be saying. Allow the Holy Spirit to confirm His voice to you. He will cause you to know that you know His voice.

Overcoming hindrances

I want to encourage you that God is speaking to you. Sometimes we can be unaware of it. I want to address some hindrances in our own thoughts to hearing from the Lord. In the testimony above, my daughter had begun to think God didn't want to talk to her or that somehow she was deficient. We need to tear down that thinking and just believe and receive.

For some believers, fear or anxiety that they may be hearing their own thoughts and receiving those thoughts as from God, is far more of an issue than fear of being led astray by the enemy's lies. It is the Spirit of God that will cause you to know that you know that you are hearing from Him. Perhaps you may not hear perfectly with none of your own thoughts mixed in 100 percent of the time. But the Holy Spirit will teach you. He will guide you. I like to use speaking in tongues as an example. Many believers, when they first speak in tongues, worry that this is just coming from themselves. If, after they've been speaking in tongues for ten years, you ask those same believers who is speaking through them, they will tell you they **know** that the Spirit of God is praying through them without any doubt. What happened to those believers? They practiced speaking with what faith they had, and the Holy Spirit did the rest. It is the same with listening to the Spirit of God inside you.

Another trap can be looking for a voice that is outside of us. I know that many people throughout history have heard the audible voice of God. Most often, however, He speaks to His people from within. He has chosen to make His home in us, and His voice will come to our minds from within us. This makes the voice of God sound to us just like our thoughts sound. Many years ago, when I was just learning to be led by the voice of God, I thought I heard Him tell me to go to the local grocery store. Once there, I was to pray for a man in a red plaid shirt and red baseball cap who had just been diagnosed with cancer. It was a dark winter night, and I never went out alone at that time, but I went. There was no man at the store fitting the description I thought I had. I came home very disappointed and somewhat angry. I asked the Lord what that was all about. He told me to get paper and pen and gave me my first lesson in hearing the voice of God. He said, "Lesson number one, when I talk to you it will sound like you. I will never use another voice to speak to you from inside you." I realized at that moment that the "voice" I had heard in my thoughts sounded like my pastor. It was his voice, his inflection; I could almost see a picture of him in my head as I received my instruction.

When you stop and think about it, what a glorious thing that God speaks from inside of you. There is no barrier. Sin has been removed because of Jesus. The atmosphere doesn't have to be just right. I could be in the most oppressive atmosphere ever and still hear His wonderful voice clearly because He is speaking from the inside of me! Just thinking about it makes me happy and makes me want to praise Him for this ingenious idea!

Most hindrances are really wrong mindsets or lies we believe about God or ourselves. At the end of this chapter, there are a few listening exercises that put us in a position to have Him remove these obstacles. Some hindrances can be as subtle as believing something untrue about why He wants to spend time talking to you. I once believed the lie that God wanted me to spend time with Him so he could fix me to be more like Jesus. I wholeheartedly threw myself into the "fix Kathy project". It rocked my world when one day, during my quiet time with Him, He asked me, "Why do you view our time together as a means to an end? I don't. For Me this is the end. This is why I died, so we could be together." I was floored! I knew that when we spend time with Him beholding Him we are changed into His likeness. Somehow that knowledge became twisted into believing that was His purpose. There were times when I did not want to deal with things, and that attitude kept me from coming to Him. How freeing to know that just being with me is His purpose. The goal of His reconciling me to Himself was and is so we could be together forever. Our times together are the end and not the means. Now we can enjoy each other forever! Starting now! This truth released me from "performance mode" and has caused me to grow and mature in Him more than in all the previous years of striving combined!

The next hindrance that I want to address is what Jesus called a hard heart. Let's look at Mark 8: 17b-18.

> *"Do you not yet perceive nor understand? Is your*
> *heart still hardened? Having eyes, do you not see?*

19

Having ears, do you not hear? And do you not remember?"

It is clear from this verse that a hardened heart can be a cause of our ears not hearing and of our failure to understand. Matthew 13:15 also underscores this.

"For the hearts of this people have grown dull. Their ears are hard of hearing and their eyes they have closed..."

Allow the Lord to search your heart. Allow Him to show you if you have hardened your heart in certain areas or if you have grown dull of hearing. Your picking up this book and wanting to hear and see in the spirit realm in order to commune with God indicates a soft heart. Hearing and obeying are a humble way of living. During His explanation of the parables, Jesus told the disciples that their ears, eyes, and understanding were blessed. I believe it was because they were coming to Him privately to ask Him to explain. They were seeking Him and going to the Source to understand the Kingdom. That indicates a soft heart, a heart to understand. If you have become dull of hearing, your hearing can be sharpened. If you have closed your eyes, you can choose to open them. This is good news!

The next thing I want to address is not a hindrance to hearing God in general, but it could be a reason for not hearing something specific that you have asked. Once when I was doing an exercise of listening, I asked the Lord to tell me what

He thought my greatest strength was. Then I asked what my greatest weakness was at that point in my life. His answer was startling. He told me my greatest strength. Then He said that He would not tell me what my weakness was, because I couldn't handle it right then. I wasn't as free and healed of wounds and lies then, and I was already feeling guilty and crummy about how often I was "blowing it." The point I want to make is this: God wanted to and did talk to me; He just didn't want to talk about what I was asking. Scripture bears this out.

> Mark 4:33 *"And with many such parables he spoke the word to them **as they were able to hear it.**"*

Isn't our God gracious and good! He is full of compassion towards us and only wants to speak for our edification. He can be trusted to never tear us down. Even in his correction He is affirming and building us up. The words He speaks to us are spirit and life. (John 6:63)

I have also discovered that He will sometimes be silent when I am pursuing Him for a specific answer because He wants to talk about something else first. In this case, I just say to the Lord, "Okay, if You don't want to talk about that, what *do* You want to talk with me about?" His answer is always forthcoming.

Let's think and declare truth

We have seen that believing lies can be a hindrance to us, so let's look at the truth and let it set us free. The banner

Scripture, or theme Scripture if you will, for the whole course is Matthew 13. There is so much to glean from this chapter that we will be referring to it many times throughout the book.

> Matthew 13:10-13 *And the disciples came and said to Him, "Why do You speak to them in parables?" He answered and said to them, "Because it has been given to you to know the mysteries of the Kingdom of Heaven, but to them it has not been given. For whoever has, to him more will be given and he will have abundance; but whoever does not have, even what he has will be taken away from him. Therefore I speak to them in parables, because seeing they do not see, and hearing they do not hear, nor do they understand.*

And skipping to verse 16: *But blessed are your eyes for they see, and your ears for they hear.*

The whole chapter, starting from verse one with the parable of the sower, is about hearing. It is about hearing the words of the Kingdom. Jesus was talking to His disciples, and that is who we are - His disciples. He said that it has been given to us to know the mysteries of the Kingdom. He said our eyes do see and are blessed because of it. He said our ears do hear and are blessed. We will hear and understand. We will be good ground and bear fruit from it. Let our confession be the same as Jesus' confession over us. Begin to declare over yourself that your ears hear, your eyes see, and it has been given to you to know the mysteries of the Kingdom!

Be careful how much you hear.

I believe the following verses show that how much we are hearing from God and understanding matters. Words are the currency of the Spirit realm. Jesus said what you hear in secret would be shouted on the rooftops. Real spiritual transactions happen when we receive His words and speak them out. Matthew 13:12 says about the words of the Kingdom:

> *"Whoever has, to him more will be given, and he will have abundance; but whoever does not have, even what he has will be taken away from him."*

In Matthew 25:29 Jesus says the same thing, only this time in the context of the parable of the talents. The corresponding verse to Matthew 13:12 in the gospel of Luke (8:18) says that we are to take heed *how* we hear. When it appears in the gospel of Mark (4:24) it says:

> *"take heed what you hear, with the same measure you use, it will be measured to you; and to you who hear, more will be given."*

We are to be "taking heed" to how, what, and how much we are receiving words of the Kingdom. Measure is a volume term. From these verses I believe Jesus was saying: "Pay attention and make sure you are hearing Me. Pay attention to how much and what you are hearing from Me, because when you do, you will have an abundance of My words that are spirit and life. The same measure you use to listen will be the measure of revelation I pour out in return."

Some methods of hearing God will seem easier to you and more natural than others. Some methods may need more practice than other methods do. For some people it may seem difficult to "tune in" at all. But one truth remains and supersedes it all. God is speaking, and He created you to receive and respond to what He is saying. Hearing God is something we need to "take heed" of and develop

Stop now and spend some time before the Lord. If you have spoken over yourself and your ability to hear God in a way that agrees with the enemy and not God, take time to break off the power of those words from your life. Let's renounce the lie that we have to be good enough or spiritual enough to hear. "I confess and repent of agreeing with the enemy concerning my ability to hear God. I cancel every assignment of the enemy against my hearing God, and I break every agreement I have made with him, by my thoughts, words or actions - in Jesus Name!"

Next, begin to proclaim that it has already been given to you to know the mysteries of the Kingdom. Proclaim: "Blessed are my eyes, for they see! Blessed are my ears, for they hear! Blessed is my understanding! Since I hear and I have His words even more will be given me, and I will have an abundance of the words of God to me. I will bear fruit from them 30, 60 and 100-fold!" I dare you to say it over yourself out loud daily. Try it and see what happens!

Listening exercises

Here are some listening exercises that you can do. When doing these exercises, we are practicing listening to the Divine flow of communication inside us. Just relax, and close your eyes if it helps. You are going to ask the Lord some questions. Don't "try" to make an answer that you are sure is God come to your mind in a certain way. Just let an answer come to your thoughts easily and write it down. Sometimes we make things harder than they have to be, and if an answer comes to our minds speedily we think it was too easy to be God.

Exercise one: Ask the Lord what He sees as your greatest strength right now. The answer is sure to surprise you. His thoughts toward us surpass our own thoughts about us. If, and *only* if, you have heard the Lord answer this question, then proceed to ask Him what He sees as your greatest weakness right now. Just focus on hearing Him from inside of yourself where He has made His home. Tune in to the divine flow of thoughts that will come to you, and write them down. When you have heard the answer to the first two questions, you could follow with asking Him how He will help you in your weakness or how you could apply that strength in your life right now. Have a conversation with God.

Exercise two: Ask the Lord: "Is there a lie I believe about You or about how You feel about me that is hindering deeper fellowship?" Again, simply focus on the fact that He is in you and will answer you from that place. The words and thoughts will "float up" to your mind. Believe that what comes to you is from God. Believe you have what you asked for.

> Matthew 7:11 *If you then, being evil, know how to give good gifts to your children, how much more will your Father who is in heaven give good things to those who ask Him!*

Check it

The answers that you received and wrote down can be evaluated and checked. Ask yourself if your answer lines up with what Scripture reveals about who God is and how He feels about you. If the answer is yes, you can be sure that the Holy Spirit is speaking to you from inside you. You could ask the Lord to give you a confirming Scripture. You could also ask a trusted, confident veteran of hearing the Lord to do some exercises with you the way I did with my daughter. The beauty in writing down what you hear is that you also can submit what you hear to others in the Body if the nature of it is contrary to what Scripture reveals. What God says through His Spirit will never be contrary to Scripture.

Chapter 2

Blessed are My Eyes!

...anoint your eyes with eye salve that you may see.

Rev 3:18b

In the first chapter, we learned about God's voice being inside of us and sounding a lot like our own thoughts. While some have heard the audible voice of God, I believe people usually experience His voice as a spontaneous flow on the inside. This internal flow can be discerned and tuned in to. Spiritual seeing works the same way. Many people have been totally enveloped in visionary experiences with the Lord and experienced what they saw so fully that they didn't know if they actually left their body or not. There are open visions where a person's eyes are open and they perceive the natural realm and a spiritual vision at the same time. But in this chapter I want to focus again on God communicating from inside you. I want you to explore your inner "mind's eye", your imagination, as a means of communing with God. There is visual communication happening all the time inside you.

Imagination, how we think and remember

The human brain is an amazing creation. Our ability to take in and process information on many levels and in many ways is a wonder. Our subconscious mind is taking in and sending out information constantly. Our conscious mind is doing the same thing. Our minds are so efficient that we don't recognize or isolate what is happening or *how*. *How* are we thinking? Our imagination, our internal image-making capacity, is a bigger part of our thinking, remembering, and experiencing of life than we know.

Our society has demeaned what we see through our imagination as fantasy. How many times have you heard, "Oh, that's just your imagination!"? We use the word imagination to indicate that something is not real or not present. It's merely a figment. We have deduced from our cultural understanding and use of the word that anything happening in the creative image-making area of our mind is not real, so no real weight or meaning can be attached to it. But when we stop to look into *how* we think and remember, we will see that the image-making part of our brain is involved in the way we process a lot of everyday information. In fact, it seems like it's our brain's preferred processor.

I want to encourage anyone who may feel uncomfortable with the idea of God or themselves using their imaginations as a means of real communication. Jesus, who is our example in everything, both heard and saw in the spirit realm. Jesus said that He only said what He heard the Father saying, and He only did what He saw the Father doing. *How* did Jesus see? Did He walk around in an open vision around the clock, or was he seeing internally? If Jesus, the Son of God, needed these ways of communication between Himself and the Father, how much more do we? There are many Scriptures, including our theme chapter, Matthew 13, that separate and delineate the spiritual senses of hearing and seeing. Why? I believe it is because we were designed to function that way. The Lord Himself is encouraging us to have both of these avenues of communication open and active. He said that we are to *live* from what we receive from these senses, and then told us that it's the *only* thing He lived from. (John 5:19 &30; John 12:49)

You have heard the saying that a picture is worth a thousand words. It really is true. Often a picture is quicker and conveys a wealth of meaning in just a flash. It is also a well-known and scientifically documented fact that the more senses that are used to convey information, the bigger and longer lasting the impact is on us. The more senses used, the greater our capacity to "experience" the information, rather than merely receiving it in a detached manner. Educators know this and long ago began using song and hand motions to teach. This is why we sing the ABC's instead of just saying them. This is why in many schools foundational math is done with manipulatives. Students count beads or pieces of macaroni that they can see and touch. Advertisers know this as well. This is why, when they attempt to sell you a car, they will try to excite your senses with ideas of wind, speed, freedom, and even sexual attraction. The more senses they use to stimulate you, the more likely you are to buy the car.

I don't think when God created our minds to work this way that He was doing it to help advertisers sell you something. I believe He did it so that we could experience Him through the wonderful blessing of our image-making capacity. This capacity allows ethereal or abstract realities to be conceptualized in the same way that taking two beads away from four helps kids conceptualize numbers.

Our minds are naturally hard-wired to think visually. Before you think, "I'm not hard-wired that way," just take a moment and do the following exercise with me. Close your eyes and think of a Coke bottle for about 3 seconds. Take time to do this now before reading on. Next, take time to remember the best vacation you ever had. Just take a few moments, close your eyes, and think about how great it was.

OK, when I asked you to remember the best vacation you ever had, how did you remember? Most of us pulled up a picture of the vacation in our mind's eye. Most of us had a moving picture complete with sounds, smells, wind, etc. . . . There were more senses involved because we experienced it. Now think about how you thought of a Coke bottle. Did you just think the words "Coke bottle, Coke bottle," over and over? Of course not! You naturally "saw" a Coke bottle in your mind's eye. Now think of your Coke bottle again. Close your eyes, and see it again. Really take a good look at it and then open your eyes. Do this now. This time you can notice detail. Try to answer the following questions from the flash of the bottle you had. Is the lid on or off? Is it cold or warm? Is it full or empty? You received all of that in the first flash you had, but now you have taken the time to notice detail and think about what you saw. It's the same with God-given pictures; we can look at them intently, ask Jesus for the meaning, notice details, and give weight to the message from God. Habakkuk 2:1 says ". . . I will **watch** to **see** what you will say to me. . ." You can allow the Spirit of God to put images on the screen of your mind as easily as you did it through the Coke bottle demonstration. You were designed by an awesome Creator to work that way. We think in pictures and store and retrieve memories in pictures. This everyday thinking is happening in your imagination. I challenge you to go against the grain of our culture and no longer say: "That's just your imagination!"

Kardia and Dianoia

Kardia and *Dianoia* are two Greek words that are translated heart and mind respectively in the New Testament. *Kardia* means the very middle of you, your mind, intellect, thoughts, and feelings. *Dianoia* means the exercise of the mind in imagining, deep thought, and understanding. Why wouldn't He who created our imaginations use them to communicate and make Himself known to us? *Kardia* is used in the New Testament 161 times. It is translated heart. *Dianoia* appears 13 times and is translated as mind, understanding, or imagination. Both of these Greek words for heart and mind have everything to do with what goes on in our heads. The great commandment (Mark 12:30) instructs us to love God with all of our hearts (*Kardia's*) and all of our minds (*Dianoia*) How do we love God with the exercising of our minds? I believe that one way He gave us to do this is by causing our imaginations to be filled with the revelation knowledge of God. Paul prayed for the Ephesians that *the eyes of their Dianoias (the exercise of their mind) would be enlightened (made to see) so they could grasp the hope of His calling, the riches of the glory of His inheritance in the saints, and what is the exceeding greatness of His power toward us who believe.* Could it be that God wants to use our mind's eye to show us all that's available to us if we believe?

> Romans 6:13 says: *And do not present your members as instruments of unrighteousness to sin, but present yourselves to God as being alive from the dead, and your members as instruments of righteousness to God.*

As we take time to present our imagination, the eyes of our heart, to the Lord as an instrument for His use, we will receive a divine flow of revelation through it. The Creator made it, and He can use it. The Lord has also given us the job of stewarding it by not presenting it as an instrument of unrighteousness to sin. We must guard our minds and keep our "eye gate" clean. We must choose the pictures we allow in our mind.

> Matthew 6:22-23 (NASB) *"The eye is the lamp of the body; so then if your eye is clear, your whole body*

will be full of light. But if your eye is bad, your whole body will be full of darkness. If then the light that is in you is darkness, how great is the darkness!"

May the visual capacity of our hearts be kept clear and not be clouded with the darkness that is in the world.

Proverbs 23:7 says, *As a man thinks in his heart, so is he...* The Hebrew word translated thinks means, "to split or open, to act as a gate keeper." The word for heart is "vitality either bodily or mentally, own person, appetites, lust etc..."

So, the Scripture could read **as a man splits the center open, to act as a gate keeper of his own vitality either bodily or mentally, so is he.** Wow! The jobs we do as gatekeepers of our minds and bodies determine our state of being. That is a very good reason to be the best gatekeepers we can be.

Our imagination belongs to us, and like our other members, *we* can use it as an instrument of righteousness. We are the gatekeepers of our minds and lives according to Proverbs. We can initiate visual conversation with God and also put ourselves in a position to receive visual communication back from Him. I have only had one "open vision" as of this writing and do not know how to initiate such a thing. But inner vision is also genuine communication from God, and I have discovered that *you can* use your imagination as an instrument to initiate and/or put yourself in a position to receive visions from the Lord.

I like to call them visual conversations. At this point many western Christians draw back and say something like: "Hold on there! I don't want to visualize anything! I want it to be all God, or I don't want anything! If I start it, then it will be me and not God." There is a fear that if you put any stock in anything you receive in such a way, you could be led into error. No one wants to be led away from sound doctrine. I exhort you though; realize *Who* is the Author and Finisher of your faith. *Who* is the One who is able to present you faultless and blameless on the day of Christ? *Who* is the One who is able to keep that which is committed to Him? You and your own understanding of doctrine are not what will keep you as the days get darker. He will. That being said, He who speaks today is He who spoke the Scriptures, and these two will always agree. What the Spirit reveals to us will always be supported by what He reveals in The Bible, which is His Word for all time, for all people.

I would like to say to anyone who is fearful of trusting the Lord to speak to them this way, "Where is your faith?" If you ask your Father for bread, will He give you a stone? If you ask God a question verbally in prayer, do you think that because you initiated the conversation that you also are making up the answer? Or do you believe that He hears you like the Bible says He does and He is the one answering you? In John 5:37-40, Jesus says to the Pharisees that they haven't heard Him or seen Him, nor do they have His words abiding in them. Jesus said this was because they did not believe, and so continued to search the Scriptures instead of coming to

Him to have life. Let's not let unbelief keep us from coming to Him who is truth and life! We need to de-mystify seeing in the Spirit. It is as simple as falling off a log! It is the way the Creator made you to function, to think, to remember. (Remember the Coke bottle.) We must believe that seeing in the Spirit is natural and not the function of a few super-spiritual people. It is not a "gift" or "level" earned, but simply a way God designed us to exchange information and come to the knowledge of Him. When we believe this we will find ourselves with a well-used, wide-open channel through which God can pour forth revelation. Just like everything else in the kingdom of God, we must have faith to receive.

Scripture shows us that our spirit man has eyes in Luke 16:19-23, in the story of the rich man and Lazarus. Verse 23 clearly says that ". . . in hell, he lifted up his eyes."

In the New Testament, Jesus says the Spirit will show you things to come. He says that the Spirit will take what is His and show it to you! (John 16:13-14)

Let's look at what Hebrews has to say in the Amplified Version.

> *Hebrews 5:11 Concerning this we have much to say which is hard to explain, since you have become dull in your spiritual hearing and sluggish even slothful in achieving spiritual insight.*

Read our theme Scripture Matthew 13:13 again, this time from the Amplified Bible.

This is the reason that I speak to them in parables: because having the power of seeing, they do not see; and having the power of hearing, they do not hear, nor do they grasp and understand.

It is clear that the seeing, the hearing, and the understanding are there for all. The indictment against the religious people of the day was that they had the power to see, but were not *using* it. But Jesus said to His disciples, "Blessed are your eyes for they see!" Knowing that it had been given to them to understand caused the disciples to go to Him for the explanation of the parable. The heart of Jesus is to have you draw near to see, to hear, and to understand. It **has been given** to you to know the mysteries of the kingdom!

Again it's worth taking time to tear down the lie that we "earn" the right to spiritual insight by being righteous enough or spiritual enough. Simply accept that it **has been given** to you already by a loving Father who wants to be with you.

Many years ago, my husband and I were taught by another couple concerning divine guidance. This was when I began to respect the different way my husband heard God. He mostly heard God through flashes of pictures and what I call "knowings." He just knew things. When I would ask, "Did God **say** that to you?" he would have trouble answering me. I heard God only in words and would write long conversations with Him in my journal. I was then dismissive of what Doug "felt" because he wouldn't say, "God said. . . ." I thought his "knowing" or "feeling" was untrustworthy when it came to receiving guidance from the Lord. Over the course of about a year, the Lord changed my mind. Not only were Doug's "knowings" and pictures right on, they were a faster way of communicating. Sometimes his visuals seemed less detailed and led to more questions than answers. As we each grew in our relationship with the Lord, we saw that God can download amazing detail in a quick flash, as with the Coke bottle. With Doug, most often this communication came in the form of a parable or symbolic pictures that conveyed the meaning of the message, rather than literal details (such as Jesus seeing Nathaniel under the fig tree). This required him to go to the Lord for further clarification, just like the disciples in our Matthew 13 Scripture.

As I grew to appreciate this form of communication, I began to pray that God would talk to me this way, too. So He did! I began to have flashes of pictures when I prayed for or ministered to someone. Then I would ask the Lord to explain them to me. As I believed the pictures were from God and not a figment of my own imagination, I started to speak out/pray out the things I was seeing. The response of those to whom I was ministering only served to re-enforce that I was hearing God! Then I began to have videos, or what I call inspired daydreams.

Once when I was in Australia, around midnight, I was unexpectedly called upon to preach the next morning. I was exhausted and went to bed without preparing, asking the Lord to wake me up early. God gave me my first "video". He woke me very early in the morning with a video in my head of myself preaching a sermon. I just watched and listened. When I arrived at the church and the time came for me to stand behind the podium, it was as though God just pushed the "play button" and I just did what I saw and heard.

Another time, I was attending a conference with some friends. As I lay on my bed at the home we were staying in, I began to daydream about ministering to a lady there that I didn't know at all. It felt like I just let my mind wander, but I had had enough experience to pay attention to what I saw myself say and do. Later, an opportunity arose to minister to this woman on the very subjects I saw in my daydream. I didn't strive to make it happen, and it wasn't exactly like in the daydream as far as location or even the level of anointing I felt. I actually felt more in the daydream! But the issues the Holy Spirit wanted to address were the same, and I knew how to minister to her needs because of it.

Listen to a testimony from a friend of mine about receiving visual communication from the Lord:

> As a wife, mother of three, and full time high school math teacher, life could get very busy. On a given day, one of my colleagues came to me with a math expression that she had been unable to factor to its most simplified form. I took the paper she handed me, told her I would take a look at it, and stuffed it in

my "take home" bag. The evening was filled with the usual activities of dinner, homework, and baths. That night as I laid my head on the pillow, I suddenly remembered Mrs. Jones' math problem. With a very fatigued cry I said, "Oh, Jesus, I forgot to look at Mrs. Jones' math problem." As soon as I breathed the request, if you can call it that, I "saw" the entire solution to the problem written out. Immediately, I decided to get up and write down what I had seen before I forgot it. This was not a simple factoring problem, but one which involved multiple steps and took almost a whole page to write out. I am not sure whether or not I would have figured it out myself, but one thing I am sure of; it would have taken me much longer to figure it out than it did for me to "see" it already done for me by the Spirit. The only way I can explain how it happened is to say that I saw it first and then my mind comprehended it. I scribbled the following note at the top of the page to my fellow teacher:"Mrs. Jones, God loves you very much. Explain later."

I want to encourage you to begin to practice the art of visual communication with the Lord. Ask Him to speak to you this way, and then begin to receive by faith. If you have presented the "eyes" of your heart, your imagination, as an instrument of sin, spend a few minutes before the Lord about this. The more we watch and guard our eye gates and our hearts, the less cluttered our minds will be. Then it will be easier to discern the Lord using our imaginations for His glory.

Can real spiritual transactions and real conversations with God happen inside our imaginations? Consider Matthew 5:28 where Jesus said that if you look at a woman with lust, you have committed the sin of adultery with her in your heart. If that is true, then we also know that other positive or negative happenings in our minds have real substance in the spirit realm. The last half of the verse says we can present our members to Him as instruments of righteousness. Let's present our ears, eyes, minds, imaginations, and understanding to Him for His use. We also need to renounce any negative words we have spoken over ourselves and our ability to "see". If you have spoken negatively, take some time to do this now.

Lord, I confess that I have limited the ways I have allowed You to speak to me. I break any agreements I have made in thought, word, or deed with the enemy about my ability to see in the spirit. I choose to agree with You that my ears and eyes are blessed to hear and see!

Here are some exercises to help you practice this method of receiving from the Lord.

Garden of the Heart Exercise

Song of Solomon says we are the Lord's well-watered garden that He takes pleasure in. I have an exercise called the "Garden of the Heart" that I learned about at a conference. I have been doing this exercise off and on through the years. I have truly learned a lot about myself and how the Lord views me through this exercise. Picture your heart as the Garden of the Lord. Invite the Lord to walk with you in your Garden and visualize the two of you there. Then just watch and listen and respond as the Holy Spirit leads you.

Here is a testimony from a friend of mine who has done this exercise many times:

"Kathy's teaching on our being God's garden has been one of the greatest blessings I have experienced in my devotional life. Often this exercise has paralleled my own spiritual growth in certain areas of my walk with the Lord. When I first began to "see" my garden, what I saw was deep rich soil with pure white roots in it and a plush green plant above ground. My first response was, "Lord, there is no fruit on this plant." It appeared to be a tomato plant, but the fruit was conspicuously missing. In the months following that exercise, the Lord did some wonderful things inside of me, setting me free from issues that I had carried for years. Then in my garden exercise, I began to see red, ripe tomatoes on my plant. In the following months as the Lord did more

41

inner healing in me, my garden expanded in size and in quantity with a variety of plants and trees. I have also perceived fountains and even a waterfall there. There is a bench there where I go and have talks with the Lord. One day as I sat on the bench, I noticed a wall around the garden with a vine growing on it. The vine was dried and appeared to be dead. When I asked the Lord about it, He replied that it represented a particular relationship in my life that I had not tended the way I should. He then shared with me that it was a relationship that He had been at work in, the vine was not dead, and I was to trust Him and listen for His voice in this relationship. As I began to trust Him in the relationship and allowed Him to make it what He desired, the vine began to become green and plush again in my garden times with Him.

Several weeks ago I was going through a very difficult time and was "beating myself up" because of something I had been unable to accomplish, and it had disappointed another person. I have found, as I think most of us have, that it has been easier to forgive others than it has been to forgive myself. One particular day, as I was starting to have a "sinking" feeling inside, I heard the Lord say, "Let's dance." That was when I discovered that there is a dance floor in my garden and My Beloved was inviting me to come be with Him there. It was so gratifying to dance with the Lord and experience His unconditional love for me and delight in me.

I love being His garden and having Him teach me and guide me with this exercise. There is just no end to His love; there is no end to His power; there is no end to all He would show us and speak to us if we are willing to visit with Him there. There is an old gospel song called "I Come to the Garden" written by C. Austin Miles about one hundred years ago. The words of that song are full of spirit and truth: "And He walks with me, and He talks with me, and He tells me I am His own, and the joy we share as we tarry there, none other has ever known." The writer of that song knew the garden experience. I am convinced it is one that He has for all of us."

Picture Scripture Exercise

Choose a scene from Scripture, such as coming to the tomb to find the stone rolled away. Ask the Lord to speak to you while you visualize the scene, and see and hear what He wants to show or tell you. Or imagine yourself walking with Jesus as He comes to town to raise Lazarus and encounters Martha and Mary and the crowds. See Him call Lazarus out. Invite the Lord to show you something about it that you didn't think about before. Another good one is to imagine yourself on the beach when Jesus cooks the disciple's breakfast, and invite Him to speak to you about that time. Remember that you may initiate the visual conversation with

God around a scene from Scripture, but you will know when the Lord takes over the scene and is speaking to you through it. I have also experienced "meeting the Lord" in a Biblical scene in my mind's eye and He said to me, "Let's go somewhere else." Then He proceeded to show me something completely different. Your goal is to be with the Lord and receive what He wants to reveal to you, not to complete or be successful at an exercise. Nor is the goal to experience the Bible story exactly the way it is written. The way it is written is the way it happened. What you are after is what the Lord would like to say to you through that scenario today. The key is to relax. Put yourself before Him and then follow where He leads.

Here is a testimony from a woman named Beth. During a church retreat workshop, she did a Scripture Picture exercise from the account of Jesus raising Lazarus.

> "In the fall of 2009, our church had a women's retreat in the mountains of North Carolina. On Saturday morning, women from our congregation led workshops that we could attend. These workshops expressed how the Lord loves us by His desire to communicate with us. In the workshop I chose, Kathy spoke of prayer and meditation in a way that I had never heard before. She encouraged us to think of a Biblical moment when Jesus walked this earth and imagine being there. I closed my eyes and

thought of the story about Lazarus, Mary and Martha's brother. Jesus arrived on the scene after Lazarus had been dead for days. I found myself right next to Jesus immediately before He commanded Lazarus to rise from the dead. In that instant, He turned around to me and said, "YOU call him forth!" I was astounded and amazed when it happened! In that moment, I knew that Jesus was telling me that I had been given all authority on this earth to see His kingdom come to pass. I am to be bold for Him and proclaim out of MY mouth the declarations of life over others. I have had a greater reality since then of how true it is that the same Spirit that raised Christ Jesus (and Lazarus) from the dead lives in ME. I can proclaim victory over the enemy in my life as well as others' lives."

**See Appendix A for several meditations on the Blood done by a friend of mine. They are another wonderful example of the richness and depth of experience with the Lord that can be had in a visual, Biblical meditation.

Chapter 3

Wake up to Dreams!

You might think "Wake up to Dreams" is a strange title for this chapter. However, I believe it really describes a process I went through in regard to dreams. A close friend of mine had been reading a book about dream interpretation in which the author stated that every dream is from God. I did not agree with that statement. It seemed to me that dreams could also be a natural outworking of our subconscious mind. I also knew that nightmares are dreams and that they do not come from God. We discussed it at length. Finally my friend asked me if I could remember a dream I had recently that I did not think was a "God dream." I'd had one, just the night before. She asked me to tell her the dream. I did. Then she proceeded to ask me a few questions. Within five minutes I knew that the dream was in fact from God, and I knew what He was saying through it. I was appalled that I was going to "throw it away" as nonsense. I was clueless that He was speaking! I had to wonder how many other nights the Lord had been trying to speak to me, and I had ignored it in my ignorance. I still would not make a statement that every dream is a message from God. What I will say, though, is this: I believe that many believers are not using dreams as a means of listening to Him, but God is using dreams as a means of speaking to them! I have been "awakened to dreams"!

Dreams are one method that God uses to speak to us today. I think many Christians don't believe that, so they don't take their dreams seriously. Others who do believe are frustrated, because, while they believe God talks to us through dreams, their dreams remain a mystery to them because they don't understand how to interpret them. Their dreams are like getting a telephone call from someone dear to them that they really want to hear from, but there is so much static on the line that they only get bits and pieces, not a clear whole message. I think it is safe to say that this is not God's intention. If He is giving you a dream, He wants you to understand it.

I believe that the emphasis in this course on developing our ability to see and hear in the Spirit will be very helpful in developing skills for dream interpretation, as well. Some dreams are literal, and therefore the meaning is more obvious and easier to understand. Other dreams are symbolic. In our Matthew chapter 13 Scripture, we know that Jesus *only* spoke to the multitude symbolically in parables. (Matthew 13:34) When the disciples heard Jesus speaking about the Kingdom in parables, they asked Him, "Why do you do talk that way?" (vs.10) Maybe they were as frustrated with their lack of understanding as some dreamers I know. Verse 35 of chapter 13 says that in parables He utters things kept secret from the foundation of the world. That is sometimes how dreams feel, isn't it? A dream can seem like a secret encoded message, difficult to decipher, but verse 36 is the key. It says that when Jesus sent the multitude away His disciples came to Him. They said, "Explain to us the parable."

Every message from God should lead us back to Him. He doesn't just desire to give you information; He desires fellowship. When the Lord speaks to you in a symbolic dream, I believe it is to cause you to come to Him for the explanation. Just like anything in the Kingdom, we receive this by *believing* that He will explain. We must believe what Jesus told the early disciples, that it has been given to us, as His disciples, to know the mysteries of the kingdom of heaven.

The Lord may use your ability to see and/or hear in the spirit to explain the dream to you. He may drop an instant "knowing" in your understanding of what the dream means. The only job we have is to come, ask, believe, and receive. This is my preferred method of dream interpretation. Some people call this prophetic dream interpretation.

What about dream dictionaries?

Dream dictionaries can be useful tools, but they can also be a hindrance. I have used them before and been successful at finding the meaning of the Lord's message with them. However, I would like to give a word of caution here. It becomes easy to rely on a book or list of symbols from a dictionary rather than the Lord. If you view dreaming as a message from the Lord, why bring in a third party book? The Lord is speaking to you; therefore He will use language that is specific to you. The imagery He uses in dreams to communicate with you will be specifically designed to speak something to you. To another person, that same imagery could mean something completely different. That is why the Lord should be the first person you go to for the interpretation, not the last. The Lord should be consulted before the symbol book. Whether found in a book or conversation with a friend, others' opinions of what things mean in the dream can be helpful or "muddy the waters".

Having difficulty?

At times it seems to me that the Lord will give me a dream that speaks to me about something that I am not willing or able to hear while I am awake. Sometimes, if a subject is fraught with high emotions, it can be difficult to simply settle down and receive the meaning. It is good to brain storm about what the elements of the dream could symbolize to you. For example, if Aunt Karen is coming to visit in your dream, and you think of her as the queen of organization, the message could be about organization coming to you and not literally Aunt Karen.

Dreaming is a means of communication about which the Lord is still teaching me. I have determined to become a better listener in this area. The more I don't dismiss my dreams as a "pizza dream", the more dreams He gives me. The more I believe that He will tell me the meaning of my dreams, the more meaning I receive from them.

Dreams can provide answers

Very real, very powerful messages full of direction from the Lord happen in dreams. An angel of the Lord came to Joseph to tell him not to be afraid to take Mary as his wife. Scripture indicates that before he fell asleep he was contemplating what he should do. He was leaning toward putting her away privately. His sought-after answer came in a dream.

> Matthew 1:18-21 *Now the birth of Jesus Christ was as follows: After His mother Mary was betrothed to Joseph, before they came together, she was found with child of the Holy Spirit. Then Joseph her husband, being a just man, and not wanting to make her a public example, was minded to put her away secretly. But while he thought about these things, behold, an angle of the Lord appeared to him in a dream, saying, "Joseph, son of David, do not be afraid to take to you Mary your wife, for that which is conceived in her is of the Holy Spirit. And she will bring forth a Son, and you shall call His name JESUS, for He will save His people from their sins.*

Did you notice the comfort and direction that came with the answer to his question about what to do? Notice the details of the future that were revealed. God is interested in communicating through dreams just as much today as he was in Joseph's time.

When my mom was a young believer, she had many questions. The Lord used a dream to answer some of them and gave her a glimpse of His future return. She has remembered this dream with anticipation for more than thirty years. She had questions about whether or not the Lord thought dancing in church was okay. She was concerned about her son's standing with the Lord. Was he ready to go if the Lord returned today? Her beautiful dream is written below:

I dreamed that there were many people gathered together on a large cement floor with partial walls and no roof. It was like a ruin from a war. I was with them. We were all trying to figure out what would be safe for us to eat because some of the food was contaminated. All of the sudden we heard a loud roaring in the distance. I looked up and saw rolling clouds with golden edges coming across the sky toward us. I yelled, "It's Jesus!" We stood and watched as the rolling clouds got closer and closer. As they were just above us they formed a half circle or horseshoe shape. A light shone through the center. I looked up and saw Jesus standing in the center. His feet were even with the clouds, and He was as tall as you could see. I thought that any second we would go and meet Him in the air. Instead, He floated down and stood in the center of us. He then walked among us and touched us and spoke to each of us. I reached up and kissed His hand. He took my hand and started dancing with me. I was in awe of that. He put His arm around my son's shoulder and said, "My, you are a big boy." I didn't recognize anyone else, but I knew everyone. Across from the people greeting Jesus were several long tables with many sad faced people sitting around them. His face was sad as He looked at them. Several women had babies in their arms. I just knew that they didn't know Jesus. I asked Jesus, "What about the babies?" He said "Go get them and bring them to Me." I went and got each baby from their mother's arms and gave them to Jesus. He gave them to women near Him. Then He looked over at the group at the table and back at us and said, "I have separated you. Stay separated until I return. I will return for you soon." I woke up and wrote it down.

The Lord used this dream to tell my mom that it was okay with Him for her to dance. He also used this to put to rest her fears over her son's readiness. He revealed how much He loves us and how sad He was that people in the one group had rejected Him. My mother felt such overwhelming love during this entire dream. Today my mom dances on her church's worship dance team and is eagerly waiting to see Him come in those rolling clouds!

Spiritual events happen in dreams

Most Christians are aware that the Lord cut a covenant with Abraham in Genesis 15. But have you ever noticed that the covenant with Abraham was cut and spoken out by the Lord in a sequence of a vision and a dream? It amazes me how something as important and foundational to our faith as the Abrahamic Covenant actually was done in a dream!

Warnings are given in dreams

Warnings of future events can happen in dreams as with Pharaoh dreaming about the famine. (Gen. 41) He had a dream in which he saw seven fat cows and seven lean cows representing seven years of plenty and seven years of famine. Notice that although Pharaoh was not serving God, the Lord still gave him the warning dream. However, he needed Joseph to tell him what the dream meant. This warning preserved the people of Israel as well as the Egyptians.

Interpretations can come over time

One night my husband and I were in our bedroom talking. We were sharing what the Lord was saying to us about living in America. We had been off the mission field for some time, but we had always thought that once the kids were grown we might be sent back by the Lord. We had finally come to the conclusion that we were supposed to be living in America for the foreseeable future. I was fully convinced of this. My actual comment to my husband before we turned out the light was: "At least we know one thing about the future!"

We went to sleep, and that night I had a dream. I dreamed that I was in an Asian city. I knew in the dream that I was a new resident there. I had that foreign feeling that I recognized and experienced when I lived abroad. In the dream a little Asian boy ran up to me and spoke to me in British English. He told me all about a Burger King that was in the city, walking distance away. He hugged me and seemed to really love me. I knew he really wanted me to meet him later at the Burger King for dinner. In the dream, my husband did not want to spend the money and had planned to cook something in our apartment. He declared that we would not go to Burger King but eat this strange meat I had never had before. I was disappointed and frustrated. But I followed him into the apartment complaining and trying to get him to take me to Burger King.

The next morning I was still frustrated. I quickly jumped to the conclusion that the Lord had given me the dream to tell me that I was going to the mission field again, this time to Asia. I told my husband that we didn't even know the one thing we thought we knew the night before! I sat and pondered before the Lord what the dream could mean. It seemed obvious to me, but I needed to hear Him say that we were going to be living in another nation again. I didn't receive any light on this for a few days, but I continued to dream. I had a total of five dreams, but with no interpretation. One day the Lord spoke to me about them without my bringing them up. All five dreams were explained by the Lord to me. They were like one long cohesive message. The part I shared above did not mean that I was going to live in Asia. The Lord was speaking to me about living in America as someone who belonged to another world. My husband represented the Holy Spirit, and the boy represented the pressure of society to "have it your way". That is the slogan for Burger King.

I learned several things from this dreaming experience from the Lord. First, I learned the importance of writing down every dream I have. If I had not written the dreams down as they came, there was no way I would have remembered the first as clearly as the last when the Holy Spirit began to give me the interpretation. I also learned patience in waiting for the interpretation to be explained to me. What if I had gotten frustrated over my lack of receiving understanding and quit writing down my dreams? What if I had quit seeking Him for the explanation? I would have robbed myself of a lot of revelation He was trying to give me.

I also learned that it is never wise to take a dream and just assume it is literal. Unless the Lord tells you it is literal, it is best to assume it is symbolic. That will keep you from assuming you know what it means and cause you to go to the Lord about it with an open mind. I believe that as we take our dreams seriously as communication from the Lord, we will dream of bright ideas, formulas, inventions, the future, and parables to unlock our hearts. The Bible is full of dreams as a method through which God spoke to His people. He is the same yesterday, today, and forever. May the people of God wake up to dreams!

Chapter 4

Other Senses. . .

Remember the illustration of the multi-lane superhighway representing various ways we can receive information from the Spirit of God? This highway is a revelation superhighway connecting heaven and earth. Heaven and earth meet in the indwelt Body of Christ. Hearing and seeing are the two main senses in the natural through which we perceive our surroundings. I believe that these two are also the main spiritual senses used to perceive what is going on in the spirit realm. You could say they are the most traveled "lanes" on the superhighway. But just like in the natural, there are many more ways to perceive and understand. These other ways of receiving revelation bring us information, just as surely as our other natural senses do. What the Lord is saying and doing can be perceived with these senses. There are many more "lanes" on this revelation superhighway. I won't even attempt to list all the ways that you can receive communication from the Lord, because I believe that the ways vary as much as the people He made vary. Our God likes variety. While this chapter is by no means exhaustive, I pray that it will do its job and open up to you many ways and means through which He may already be speaking to you.

Also I pray that this course will cause you to ask the Lord to speak in ways you have never experienced before.

Spontaneous thoughts

One of the ways or "lanes" that sometimes goes unnoticed is a spontaneous thought. This may not be conversational, and it may be hard to detect where it comes from. Have you ever had a thought that you should call a friend, only to later find out that the friend really needed to talk to you at just that moment? I call these inspired thoughts. They are timely ideas inspired by the Lord.

When my husband and I were first married, we really didn't take very good care of our cars. My husband was driving the better one to work one day, the one that was "mine". Before he started the car he had a random thought that he hadn't checked the oil in this car for quite some time. He pulled out and was driving for several minutes when he had the thought that he needed to check the oil in the car *now*. But he was running late, so he told himself he would check it on the way home and started to get on the highway. Then, right there on the entrance ramp, my car seized up and died! No oil. After the car died, it occurred to him that maybe those random thoughts were from the Lord trying to warn him. Why it wasn't more conversational like: "This is God! Stop the car! Check the oil!" I don't know. We have since learned to let these seemingly random spontaneous thoughts encourage us to inquire of the Lord. "Lord, are you saying something to me?"

The sense of smell

Sometimes the Lord wants to communicate that He is present to do certain things by using our sense of smell. In the early years of my walk with the Lord, I knew a woman who would "smell Him" frequently. I used to think that maybe she was only smelling other women's perfume in church. It seemed odd to me. Why would He do it? Occasionally through the years I would smell a wonderful fragrance during church, but I was always afraid to believe it was the Lord and not some lady behind me putting on hand cream. Now I know without a shadow of a doubt that the Lord communicates His Presence at times through our sense of smell.

My husband and I were in Poland visiting two other missionary families. These were our friends. All three of us couples had experienced some really tough times on the field and were battling with discouragement. We had just finished dinner together, and all the children were in another part of the house. While we were still at the table my husband started sniffing and asked, "Do you smell that?" We all said no. We continued clearing the table and talking about playing a game. Doug insisted several times that he smelled something similar to the anointing oil that we were all familiar with. A brother from our church made his own, with his own recipe. It had a *very, very* strong, distinctive smell! For a while no one else smelled it.

My husband went around sniffing the plug-in air fresheners in the house and all the unlit candles. None of them were producing the smell. We had moved into the living room area and were starting to play. Eventually one of the other women said, "I smell it now, too!" It had started to become a joke with us as we said, "You're just smelling so and so's feet." My husband got very still and began to address the Lord and to repent for not realizing He wanted our attention. As soon as he began to pray we were all engulfed in the Glory of the Lord. His Presence and the smell of the anointing oil were everywhere! We basked in His Presence for the rest of the evening, enjoying Him, prophesying to one another, and being encouraged. We were all changed and encouraged in His unexpected Presence that night!

Natural signs

You know, a beautiful thing about the Lord is that He can use anything! If He can use a donkey to speak, He can also use a sign, a billboard, a car, even a crack in the sidewalk to speak to you. I used to have a friend who seemed to think absolutely *everything* was a sign from God! I secretly thought she was a little flaky. What I couldn't deny, though, was the huge number of unexplainable "coincidences" that happened wherever she went. There were too many things that lined up for it to be coincidence. What I now believe is that this is the way she was listening. This is one way she expected to hear from the Lord, and so He used everyday things to speak to her. I made up my mind that if this is one way God speaks, then it will be one way that I listen. I told the Lord that He could speak to me this way, too.

It wasn't long before my eye was being caught by writing on the side of vehicles. The Lord began saying, "See that?", or I just somehow knew it was the Lord saying something to me. I then began a dialogue with Him about the things I was seeing. I have learned a great deal from the Lord this way. The more open to it I was, the more communication I received this way. Odd things happened, just like they did for my friend. One day I was driving home on a road with a speed limit of 55 mph. As I was driving, a dove came and flew right next to my driver's side window. I never looked to see exactly how fast I was going, but I didn't know birds could fly *that* fast. This pure white bird stayed with me, level with my driver's side window, for an incredibly, freakishly, long time! On and on we went down the road together. The Lord used this "sign" to speak to me about His Spirit. Just remembering how He sent that bird to fly beside me makes me feel special.

My sister was going through a very rough time a few years ago. She was at a place in her life where she didn't know if everything would be all right ever again. She was walking in the woods, trying to find some peace and stress relief, when she saw three fawns. When she saw them she knew that the

Lord was communicating to her that everything was going to be all right. There is new life.

I want to encourage you to be open for the Lord to draw your attention to Him through natural things. Remember in Matthew chapter 13, the Lord says that whoever has, more will be given to them. This is pertaining to the words or communication of the Kingdom. If you start to look for the Lord to communicate with you this way, don't be surprised when He does. Then don't be surprised if, before long, almost everything you see seems to be a message from the Lord! The Matthew 13 Scripture not only says more will be given, but it will be given in abundance. Don't think it odd; you are experiencing a scriptural principle. Do some people make this stuff up in an effort to appear spiritual before others? Probably. Should this keep us from letting the Lord use natural things to speak to us? Absolutely not!

Sense of touch

Many times the Spirit will use our sense of touch as a method to communicate a "word of knowledge". For instance, if you are praying for someone and suddenly your knee hurts for no reason, you might ask the person you are praying for if they have a knee problem.

My husband has an interesting testimony about a time the Lord used his body to tell him when someone was lying. He had a meeting with a church leader in another nation. This leader was promising my husband certain things in exchange for our ministry committing to work with him from his ministry base. This would have meant leasing property from him, and we were not sure we could trust him to do all that he was saying. As Doug was trying to discern if he should trust the man or not, God said to Doug "Hey, look at this!" My husband noticed that his left hand would get icy cold during some of the promises the man was making. Then, during some other statements, his right hand would burn. Soon he was able to discern that the Holy Spirit was making his body into a lie detector! When the man lied, Doug's left hand was cold and when the man told the truth Doug's right hand was hot! Doug was so distracted with the Holy Spirit's lie detector that what would have been a difficult meeting actually seemed like fun, as the Holy Spirit taught him that he did not have to lean on his own understanding. This is an interesting application of

> Hebrews 5:14 *"But solid food is for the mature, who because of practice have their senses trained to discern good and evil." (NASB)*

"Knowing "

Sometimes you just know things. Both my mother and my husband frequently have what they call instant "knowings". They will just look at someone and suddenly know something about them. One day I went to visit my mother to tell her that my husband and I were thinking of going on the mission field. We had not told anyone. As soon as I asked, "Guess what?" she had an instant knowing and replied, "You and Doug are going to be missionaries." She did not know it before that point. It just came to her, and she knew. I have sometimes had "knowings" when I am praying or ministering to someone. I then begin to pray along the lines of what I think I know. More often than not, the person will say, "You prayed just the right thing! How did you know?"

This is called "word of knowledge" in the list of spiritual gifts in Corinthians. Some people have the Spirit reveal minute details such as person's address, what they had for breakfast, and what they thought about on Tuesday. The purpose of this is to convince the person that God knows them and is speaking to them. This is a very cool gift that I believe can be developed as we learn to listen to the revelation He is pouring out. I have seen this form of communication from the Holy Spirit develop in my own life, though not to the point that it will in the future. I am on a journey to hear from Him however and whenever I can. Will you join me?

You can hear the Lord speak to you in something someone says, even an unsaved person. You can hear the Lord speak to you through a song, a Scripture, or a feeling of peace. There are so many ways and places to receive what He is saying, and there are so many life changing ways to use what we receive.

Listening Exercises:

1. Ask the Lord to speak to you with one of the methods that you have not experienced before. Expect Him to give you what you asked, and be an alert, ready listener.

2. Ask the Lord if there is a way that He has desired to speak to you, but you haven't been listening. Write down what He says/shows you.

3. Ask the Lord if there is a lie you have believed concerning any of these methods of communication. If He shows you something, ask Him what is the truth concerning that method.

In the next portion of this book, I will address some practical ways we can apply the methods of hearing God in our lives. These include prayer, behavior changes through brain training, inner healing, and ministry first to yourself and then to others.

Chapter 5

Brain Training

I think every Christian can identify with Paul as he agonizes over how he seems to act against his will in Romans chapter 7 & 8. The things he wants to do, he doesn't end up doing. In fact, the things he definitely doesn't want to do, that's what he does. However, Paul doesn't leave us there, with a helpless feeling. There is no, "Oh, well. . . I can't help it . . . life goes on" mentality expressed by Paul. Not only does he rejoice knowing that Jesus has separated the real him from all that sin, but he also says that, by the Spirit, we who are in the Spirit do put to death the deeds of the flesh in our bodies. Here is where we born-again Christians often trip up. Many of us have trusted the Lord to cleanse us from all unrighteousness. But after salvation, somehow we begin to think it's our job to clean ourselves/change ourselves from that point on. Let's look at the verse:

> *Romans 8:13 For if **you** live according to the flesh you will die; but if **by the** Spirit **you** put to death the deeds of the body, you will live.*

At first glance, it seems that Paul is putting the effort and responsibility back on us and himself. Let's look at verse 13 in light of verses 3 & 4 of the same chapter:

Romans 8:3-4 *For what the law could not do in that it was weak through the flesh, God did by sending His own Son in the likeness of sinful flesh on account of sin: He condemned sin in the flesh, that the righteous requirement of the law might be fulfilled in us who do not walk according to the flesh but according to the Spirit.*

In the light of both of these Scriptures, it's clear that Christ already put to death the deeds of the flesh in His death on the cross. We do it by the Spirit, simply by being in Christ and appropriating what He has already done. Living according to the flesh or by the Spirit is not about behavior but about the place from which you live or more accurately, from *Whom* you live. I thank God that life and death are not decided for me by adhering to certain behaviors, but that eternal life is simply accepted.

So what is there left to do? How can we change? Praise the Lord! He left nothing unprovided for; by the power of the Spirit we can live lives that glorify Him. He, in His infinite wisdom, thought of everything. The only thing left for us to do is accept and appropriate what He has done and be transformed. We do this by meditating on what He has done and on who we are "in Christ". What He has done is all we need to put to death the deeds of our flesh. What He has done for us by moving us from the kingdom of darkness into the kingdom of light is so VAST, so incomprehensible in its awesomeness! We need the Spirit to show us all the things we have been freely given. (1 Cor. 2:12) Once we have revelation and know what has come with this glorious salvation, the Spirit also causes us to be able to appropriate it. The Spirit does this by gracing us with understanding and causing us to have our minds renewed in the knowledge of Him.

Our brains need to be renewed, and we need revelation by the Spirit. We need the Spirit who searches the deep things of God to show them to us in order to do it. That is why seeing and hearing from God are essential to having a renewed mind. Right believing begets right thinking which, in turn, begets right speaking and right actions. That equals transformation. Scripture says that when we behold Him as in a mirror, we are being changed into that same image, from glory to glory. Think about the phrase "as in a mirror." Why not say, "as we behold Him," period? Why "as in a mirror"? Because we need to behold Him in us! We need to see who we are in Him and what we possess because of Him. We must see the finished work of the cross when we look inward and evaluate ourselves. Let's look at two Scriptures which speak of looking in mirrors.

> 2 Corinthians 3:17-18 *Now the Lord is the Spirit; and where the Spirit of the Lord is, there is liberty. But we all, with unveiled face, beholding **as in a mirror** the glory of the Lord, are being transformed into the same image from glory to glory, just as by the Spirit of the Lord.*

James 1:23-25 *For if anyone is a **hearer** of the word and not a doer, he is like a man **observing his natural face in a mirror**; for he observes himself, goes away and immediately forgets what kind of man he was. But he who **looks into** the perfect law of liberty and continues in it, and is not a forgetful **hearer** but a doer of the work, this one will be blessed in what he does.*

Wow! What a different outcome based on what you look at when you see yourself. One example is looking at the Lord in us, and one is looking just at our natural face. I believe looking at the natural face equates to judging ourselves by focusing on our own abilities or lack thereof, on our weaknesses or sin. We go away from looking at ourselves through that filter and forget who we really are in Christ! I believe there is a key here in these two verses. James likens the one who hears the word but is not a doer to someone only looking at their natural face. Could looking at those weaknesses keep someone in a cycle of hearing and not doing? I believe so. But the ones who look at the Lord in themselves are the ones transformed into His image! The difference is what you are focusing on and consequently believe about yourself. I like how James calls it looking into the perfect law of liberty. That one hears and does. That one will be blessed in what he does. Right here is a key to becoming transformed by the renewing of our minds. Believe you are who He has said you are! Persisting and continuing to see Him in you, it's the hope of Glory. First you believe, and then your behavior follows. What do **you** see when you look at **yourself**?

How many of you have tried to be better and curb some behavior in yourself through chastising yourself over and over? How many times have you concentrated on your failure and berated yourself about it? This is the adult version of your giving yourself a spanking. Did it help? Were you able to change your habits for more than a few weeks? If you are like most people, the verbal or emotional spanking probably did not bring lasting change. We were not designed that way. It's the kindness of God that draws us to repentance, not the flogging of God. It's looking into the perfected, already-done work of liberty **in you** that changes and transforms.

Doing the same thing over and over again and hoping for a different result is what Einstein said was the definition of insanity. How about we give the Lord's way a try? Everything in this kingdom to which we have been called seems to operate in a way that is contrary to the laws of our natural mind. Why not believe **we are** first and then our actions will naturally follow our identity? Why not look at who you are in the light of His face? If you belong to Him, **you are** holy. **You are** the righteousness of God in Christ. **You are** born of an incorruptible seed. We are righteous so we do deeds of righteousness; we don't perform righteous deeds to become righteous. When we believe we are who He says we are and continue to "look at it" or meditate on it, then our behavior will line up and manifest who we really are. We will be transformed into His image from glory to glory.

Even in the natural, if a parent tells a child that he is a good boy, he will live up to it. He may not do it perfectly, but if he believes he **is** good, he naturally wants to **do** good things. If a parent tells a child he is bad, and the child believes it, then he will show you how bad he can be. How many of us are telling ourselves who we really are so we can believe it and live up to it? How many of us can be comfortable saying to ourselves in a mirror, "I am holy", without a little cringe?

Scripture is clear that we are to avoid being conformed to the image of this world and to be transformed into His image by the renewing of our mind, our thought processes. Changing what you think can seem like a big and overwhelming job. Let's remember that He wouldn't tell us to do something that He wasn't ready to do for us from the inside of us. Remember the Scripture says we are transformed "just as by the Spirit". He -The Spirit- is the transformer. We just have to yield our minds. I want to share with you some practical ways to do that.

Colossians 3:10 says we have ...*put on the new man who is renewed in knowledge according to the image of Him who created him.* That is interesting. This new man is renewed with knowledge that is according to His image. It sounds like our mirror Scripture from earlier. When we look at His Image in us we are changed into the same image by the Spirit. The words used in these Scriptures, such as look and image, are visual. It is important to have a personal, inner picture of yourself that lines up with God's image of you. Bill Johnson often says, "I can't afford to have a thought in my head about me that He doesn't think about me." I would take this one step further and say that it is important to make sure your mental concept or view of yourself that is not expressed in words, but somehow deeper than words or conscious thoughts, lines up with His picture or image of you.

You might be asking, "Can it be that simple? Can I really get rid of this sinful behavior pattern I've felt trapped in by meditating on Jesus and the truth that He has made me righteous?" It seems too good to be true that we don't have to major on our weakness to be made strong in that area. It seems counterintuitive to our natural mind that focusing on something and someone else would be what deeply changes us. You might be wondering if you can really believe this based on the two Scriptures about mirrors, so let's look at another Scripture that talks about forgetting what kind of man we are.

> II Peter 1: 8-9 *But also for this very reason, giving all diligence, add to your faith virtue, to virtue knowledge, to knowledge self-control, to self-control perseverance, to perseverance godliness, to godliness brotherly kindness, and to brotherly kindness love. For if these things are yours and abound, you will be neither barren nor unfruitful in the knowledge of our Lord Jesus Christ. For he who*

*lacks these things is shortsighted, even to blindness, and has **forgotten that he was cleansed** from his old sins.*

W. E. Vine's *An Expository Dictionary of New Testament Words* says shortsightedness in this verse "does not contradict the preceding word 'blind,' it qualifies it; he of whom [this blindness] is true is blind in that he cannot discern spiritual things, he is nearsighted in that he is occupied in regarding worldly affairs", or in other words, the shortsighted person is focusing on what he sees with his natural eyes and not looking with his spiritual eyes. He is looking at his natural face, and forgets what kind of man he is.

We are to grow in the knowledge of Christ. When we do we will be partakers of His nature and add these fruits of the Spirit who is now living in us. The one who lacks these fruits according to verse 9 is the one who has **forgotten** that he was cleansed. Peter goes on to say in verses 10-15 that for this reason he will constantly **remind** believers of the truth they already received and are firmly established in. He went so far as to tell them that he would ensure they are **reminded** even after he was dead! I think it's safe to say Peter thought constantly remembering that they have been made righteous through Jesus was vital for the believers to manifest who they really were.

I believe that if we stop, for instance, trying to be more patient, and instead marinate in what it means to be "in Christ" we will as a consequence become more patient.

However, we can also use our ability to hear and see in the Spirit to become more intentional in living from our identity in specific areas.

This brings me to an exercise that can be very effective in renewing our minds. We can purposefully take a situation where we continually display a nature that is contrary to our new man, our true self, and change our responses. We can ask the Holy Spirit to show us what it would look, sound, and feel like to be displaying His image in that situation. Seeing yourself doing it His way is another way to see His image in you.

For example, let's say I have teenagers who act or speak in a certain way that evokes anger or fear reactions from me. I could ask the Holy Spirit, "What would that situation look like when my teenagers 'push that button' and I react like You would?" Then we need to **see** it. We need to "experience" ourselves acting out of the new man that is according to His image. Be specific. See the scenario in your mind's eye. Allow the Holy Spirit to "show" you in your imaginative scenario what it looks, sounds, and feels like to act out of your true identity. What does His image look like in that situation though you? Experiencing the scenario with you perfectly displaying His image will greatly increase the likelihood of your acting from your identity when your teenager is in front of you. This is one great way to apply hearing and seeing in the Spirit to your life. Spending a little time intentionally daydreaming with the Holy Spirit can change your life!

Think without mixture

Sometimes, as well-educated Christians with excellent Bible doctrine, all our knowledge creates a problem. Have you ever tried to counsel a fellow Christian who was having problems, and their response to everything you said was, "I know, I know." Yet with all their knowing, their problem remains. We can know something, and have mental assent that what we know is true, but also have experiential knowledge screaming or whispering a different "truth" from somewhere inside us. For example, I know that Jesus heals sickness and disease. I know the verse that says by His stripes we are healed. I might know this on the level of giving mental assent and agreement that this is true. I agree that I will lay hands on the sick and they will recover. Then, when faced with someone in front of me dying of cancer, I may have another subconscious or conscious "knowledge" that the last person I prayed for with cancer died. This can hinder me from believing for a different outcome. I call this "experiential knowledge". This experience is factual, but it's not truth.

I said subconscious or conscious earlier because sometimes you know what you are thinking and other times it is so subtle you don't realize that there is an inward part of you that does not agree with the Word. As a matter of fact, I think one of satan's most used weapons is the weapon of lying experiences. A better way to say it would be lies that spring from our experiences. In our mind and emotions, the conclusions we draw from our experiences can look like truth.

As a matter of fact, the more experiential something is the more true it seems. So we have a war: experiential "facts" lying to us versus the truth of the Word. This is what James referred to as being double-minded.

> James 1:6-8 *But let him ask in faith, with no doubting, for he who doubts is like a wave of the sea driven, and tossed by the wind. For let not that man suppose that he will receive anything from the Lord; he is a double-minded man, unstable in all his ways.*

James says that a double-minded man isn't in a position to receive anything from the Lord. Faith is what is required to receive in the Kingdom we live and move in. James says faith with no doubting. There should be no mixture of truth and lies. Many of us have a mixture in our minds similar to the example I gave about healing. Before we can Brain Train, we have to know what areas need mixture uprooted. I know that after being a Christian for over 30 years, I didn't want to believe that I had any doubts mixing with my faith, but the Lord in His mercy showed me otherwise. Get rid of the doubt, get rid of the defeat. Faith, with no doubting, is ALWAYS the substance of things hoped for.

Be a thought detective

I got the concept for what I call "The double-mindedness detection tool" from Gregory A. Boyd in his book entitled *Seeing is Believing*. I have found this to be very effective for finding out what I really believe. It goes something like this.

You say to your soul, out loud, a verse of Scripture in a short personal way. Then you quietly wait for your soul's response. I will give you an example from my own experience with this. Before I had a deeper revelation of Romans 7 & 8, I frequently struggled with condemnation. I said "Soul! Listen up! There is no condemnation for me any longer. Because of Christ I have no condemnation." And then I waited for my soul's response. It was just a little feeling of hesitation that I felt. It was just a little feeling, not a full blown thought. But when I paid attention to it, I knew that this did not seem true in my emotions, because I often felt condemned. I began to meditate on what it means to be "in Christ" over the following months. Then one day as I read Romans 7 & 8 over and over again, I got it! I really got it!! I no longer have a mixture of head knowledge and experience. Now I have freedom!

You try it. Maybe you never have spoken or listened to your own soul before, but it is not weird, it is Biblical. David spoke to his own soul repeatedly in the psalms, as though his soul were another person. Maybe David knew something we have forgotten. He even asked his soul, "Why are you down-cast within me?" and encouraged himself, "Have hope in God." Why should we not do the same? Are you ready to try?

Double-mindedness detection tool

You can use this tool anytime, with any Scripture or truth statement based on the Word of God. Just say it out loud to your soul like the example above, and listen to your soul's

80

response. You might have a feeling, a thought, or a memory surface. It might be very subtle or quite dramatic. Don't hurry through it. Really take time to listen for your soul's response. I think this is a fun and accurate way to detect any mixture of doubt within us. Here are some sample Scriptures that might help you get started:

> Romans 8:1- "Soul. Listen up! I have now no condemnation."

> Zeph. 3:17- "Soul. Listen up! The Lord dances and celebrates me with singing. I make him happy."

> Romans 8:37-"Soul! Listen up! I am more than a conqueror."

> Matt. 28:20-"Soul! Listen up! I am never alone."

Proclaim what you believe

As the currency of the Kingdom, words have power. Once we have belief without mixture and have thoughts that persist in seeing His image in us, then what we say is changed. When that happens EVERYTHING is changed. Scriptures says if we declare a thing it will be established. It also says that if we believe when we ask or speak, we will have whatever we say or have asked. That is some pretty potent stuff. Out of the abundance of our heart our mouth speaks. Brain Training is everything because it's the foundation and the power behind what we say. If God's words to us and from us are the currency through which spiritual transactions are made, then faith is the gold that backs that up and makes it worth anything. Right believing makes for right thinking. Right thinking makes for right speaking.

I know that this Brain Training really works and have been working on training my brain to know and believe who I am in Christ. The whole earth is groaning for the revealing of the sons of God. We must let our true nature be manifest. I have a recent example of this happening in me.

I had been saturating myself with the truth that, "Blessed are my ears, they hear. Blessed are my eyes, they see. Blessed is my understanding, it is made to see. I am a spiritual person who is able to discern spiritual things, by the Spirit of God." I would say and think it often. I would hear it because I said it out loud. I would read it. I experienced an increase of these things in my life and even declared, without conscious thought, to someone that I was a spiritual person who could discern spiritual things by the Spirit. When I said that so unthinkingly, with no qualification or false humility attached, that's when I knew that I really believed it. I knew I had renewed my mind in this area.

The revelation superhighway God wants to build through you starts with receiving communication from Him in the Spirit and proceeds out of your mouth to build the Kingdom. Kingdom building starts with building up the inside of you!

Chapter 6

Praying in the Spirit

What is it?

Prayer is simply communication with God. In essence this whole course is on prayer. Learning to hear him in various ways and receive from Him is half, if not more than half, of prayer. Yet in many born-again believers' prayer life, God is not given the larger part of the time to reveal, direct, and speak. Many of us have a long list of our own prayer requests, and everyone else we know is adding to its length daily with their requests for prayer. Soon prayer becomes a burdensome process during which we find ourselves "reminding God" of what He needs to do in each situation. Have you ever felt that your prayers have been reduced to vain repetition? Have you ever felt like you were twisting God's arm so He will do what He is supposed to already want to do? Have you ever felt like you prayed for dire situations with more hopeful pleading than faith? Have you ever felt like you didn't pray hard enough, earnestly enough, or long enough for a situation? Have you carried guilt and "what-if I only did more?" thoughts, causing performance pressure? If any of these questions have a "yes" answer to them, or if prayer has somehow become a boring duty to you, then this chapter will be a catalyst for life and liberty to be poured into your prayer experience!

What is praying "in the Spirit"? We know that we are "in the Spirit" because we are in Christ. According to the *Strong's Concordance* the word *in* is defined as "denoting a fixed position in time, space, or place". I believe that we could properly define praying "in the Spirit" as praying from a fixed position of the Spirit. It's not only praying with His divine perspective, but also allowing the Spirit to originate your prayers. When the Holy Spirit is the creator and power behind prayer *that* is when you are praying "in the Spirit".

Praying in other tongues is a great way to pray in the Spirit. Scripture says when you do this your intellect is unfruitful. This kind of prayer is totally bypassing your mind, because you don't understand what's being spoken. Paul prayed in other tongues so much that he could confidently say, "I thank my God that I pray in tongues more than you all." He must have been almost constantly praying in other tongues to be so confident. From my own experience, I know that allowing the Holy Spirit to have time and voice to speak over and pray for me is the single most powerful gift in my life. My aim is to be able to say with Paul that I thank God I pray in tongues more than you all!

I believe, however, that as we lay our mind down by not considering understanding or reason the highest priority in prayer; we can pray in English and still be praying in and from the Spirit. It is an exercise in humility to acknowledge that the Spirit is greater than our understanding. To not limit what He wants to do by putting our understanding on it is a challenge but not impossible. I will give you an example of praying a Spirit-created prayer in English with absolutely no understanding.

One day I was alone at a friend's house in Germany, and another friend had e-mailed from Thailand requesting prayer. These friends are great missionaries to Thailand and doing a wonderful work there. The wife explained that her husband was going through something and asked for prayer. Since I didn't know any particulars but wanted to send something encouraging to them from the Lord, I began to pray in tongues. I did this for a few minutes and then, without any reason that I knew of, I began to say in English, "He is a city on a hill." I said this over and over and then had a picture of a lighted city on a hill at night. That's all I got. No reason, no explanation, nothing else, just: "He is a city on a hill." I had a limited time to be on the Internet, so I wrote back what little I had right away. I added some of my own thoughts and a word of encouragement to the e-mail because I thought that "He is a city on a hill" was just not that encouraging. Then, because I had been taught that you don't have to understand, and that it's in fact better not to, I deleted most of my add-on's and pushed the send button. Later I got back a most astonishing e-mail from my friend. It seems she had sent out the e-mail requesting prayer to a trusted few. One of the others who got the e-mail heard the Lord direct her to look up the meaning of the man's full name on the Internet. She did so, and guess what it means? His name means "city on a hill"! She also gave him a word about being a light where he was. My e-mail was confirmation for him that God was calling him this. God was giving him this identity. It was not just something his mother had named him. This gave my friend the encouragement he needed from the Lord. He changed his name from the short form to the long form of his name from that time on. Isn't God good? The point I want to make is this: nothing I might have added with my limited understanding really made any difference. The only thing that mattered and is remembered by my friend is the one thing that came from the Spirit of God. He is a city on a hill.

> 1 Corinthians 14:14-15 *For if I pray in a tongue, my spirit prays, but my understanding is unfruitful. What is the conclusion then? I will pray with the spirit, and I will also pray with the understanding. I will sing with the spirit, and I will also sing with the understanding.*

This verse shows that we can pray from both our spirits and from our souls. The Lord wants us to pray from both. Our souls are the seat of our emotions, intellect, and will. The above verse calls it our understanding. I was encouraged by the one who taught me to follow the Holy Spirit in prayer to never resort to praying from the soul realm when I could pray from the Sprit realm instead. This is good advice, but the way I understood this became a stumbling block to me. I felt that I could not pray about my own concerns because those were soulish. The Lord gently corrected me and brought me to several Scriptures where He exhorts us to cast our cares on Him because He cares for us. The Lord wants us to unburden our souls to Him in prayer. I also know that He does not want to leave us there in the soul realm. When we are praying out of our emotions, for instance, He listens and cares. Then He gives us His own perspective and His own feelings on the matter. Then we can begin to pray from the Spirit.

Most of us know how to pray from our soul, or intellect. Some believers spend most of their prayer time praying from that place. It is praying from our souls *only* that can create a kind of boredom or sense of duty in prayer. Praying from our understanding is often a response to what is going on around us. Someone is sick, so we pray for healing. Someone is grieving, we pray for comfort. We are going around after the devil steals, kills, or destroys and doing "clean-up" prayers. In these instances, who is directing your prayer life? These prayers are defensive prayers. Prayers that begin in the Spirit are prayers of advance and attack. Paul prayed both kinds of prayers.

When what to pray and the unction to express it come from the Spirit of God, you have His words.

> Ephesians 6: 17-18 *"And take the helmet of salvation, and the sword of the Spirit, which is the word of God; praying always with all kinds of prayer and supplication in the spirit, being watchful to this*

end with all perseverance and supplication for all the
saints-"

Most of us are familiar with the Scriptures about putting on the armor of God, but have you ever connected them with prayer? This verse says to take the sword of the Spirit, which is the Word, the utterance of God; *Praying* always. . . We are to first receive or hear what He is saying and then take that sword of the Spirit and pray!! This prayer seems to have an offensive stance and not a defensive stance. It is powerful and effective. When you pray from this place, who is in control of your prayer life? The Spirit! This kind of prayer is so ground-taking in nature that you will not only pray about your now but also your future! You won't be praying in response to things, but things will be lining up and responding to your prayer. John says that the Holy Spirit will show you things to come. When He does, you are forearmed with the sword and can pray heaven down into your future.

Let's look at what Jesus said about having His words before we pray in John 15:7 *"If you abide in Me, and My words abide in you, you will ask what you desire, and it shall be done for you."* Asking is prayer. If we have His words, and from that place of being "in the Spirit" or "in Christ" we ask, then we will have it. We abide in Him, His words dwell in us, and then we ask. Not only that, but it is the formula for answered prayer. We can have confidence that we have what we asked because we know it did not originate with us but with Him. You have confidence that Jesus' prayers were answered while He was on earth. When His words abide in you and He is initiating the prayer, you can have that same confidence that your prayers will be answered as well! Look at verse 8 of John 15, *"By this* (answered prayer) *My Father is glorified, that you bear much fruit; so you will be My disciples."*

Where the Spirit of the Lord is there is liberty!

When we pray Spirit created and Spirit led prayers we are free from so many traps the enemy sets for our prayer lives. Not the least of these is boredom. If you don't know what *He* is going to say, then you don't know what *you* are going to say. Every time in the prayer closet is a new and adventurous time of learning to follow His lead. He leads by what I like to call "unction" in prayer. Paul called it "utterance". Some call it the "anointing". No matter what you call it, it is that way in which the Holy Spirit lets you know that you are pleasing Him and right on track with Him. Sometimes in prayer this unction comes on you, and you know that you are praying out in agreement with heaven. Then sometimes it lifts, yet you just know that you haven't "prayed through" on the subject. What happened? I believe that many times this is the Holy Spirit's way of telling you that you have stopped following Him and started praying out of your understanding. If you just go back to the place in prayer you last felt the anointing and begin praying there again, you will find the anointing for prayer waiting for you. In this way the Spirit teaches us to follow Him in prayer and not lean on our own understanding. This takes time, but He is an awesome, patient, forgiving teacher!

Tired of saying the same thing?

Hearing and seeing in the Spirit as we follow Him in prayer not only relieves us of boredom but also of vain repetitions. Many times these repetitious prayers stem from the feeling that our part in prayer is to convince Him to do something the Bible already tells us He wants to do.   Sometimes we find ourselves praying from our understanding and, for instance, saying daily, "God save Uncle Joe". We may come up with variations like: "Cause Uncle Joe to see he needs You," but repeat the same request over and over again. How liberating to instead say: "I know you want Uncle Joe saved; show me what to pray." How empowering to be able to receive information from God about him that only God knows. Maybe He would show you a picture of what is blinding Uncle Joe or tell you what fear is keeping him from committing to God. The Lord could show you many things to agree with heaven on for unbinding this man so he can come to the Lord.   Another possibility is that Holy Spirit would bypass your understanding altogether and intercede for Uncle Joe with groaning that cannot be uttered.   When we pray in the Spirit, whether in English or in other tongues, our faith is raised, because we know that we are praying and speaking His words over Uncle Joe. If we ask in faith, we know we have what we have asked. It is by this kind of answered prayer that we glorify God and bear much fruit. Opening ourselves up for revelation from heaven on any subject makes prayer a wonderful, intimate, and interesting time with the Lord. It produces a feeling of oneness and partnership with the Lord instead of the feeling of "twisting His arm."

Praying in the Spirit fills you with faith.

A big part of renewing our prayer life from "lifeless prayers", filled with more longing than actual faith, is renewing our minds. Have you ever left a prayer meeting more down than when you came in? I have. I have noticed that a heavy unbelief blankets these meetings when the focus is on the problems and a deep longing for the answer. This can happen when we are praying out of our souls. When we are praying from our own perspective, focused on problems and not seeing what the Lord sees, we open the door to unbelief. When this is the case, faith goes out the window, and when there is no answer to the prayer, hope quickly follows it. If you recognize this in your prayer life, I encourage you to practice the art of hearing and seeing and gaining revelation from Him before you pray. It will rock your world! Prayer will become the most fun, faith-filled adventure. You will see answers to the prayers He prays through you.

No more guilt

Following the Spirit in prayer also delivers you from the guilt and condemnation of not praying for something, or not praying enough or diligently enough etc. . . . . When you follow the Spirit you are trusting and leaning on Him and not on your own strength. You are trusting in His goodness and His ability to know what needs to be done or said. I know many people who are bound by their prayer list. They carry a heavy burden to make sure everyone is mentioned before the Lord daily. If the Lord has instructed you to make a list, I pray that you are doing it and praying about the things on the list with the power of the Spirit. I have seen that sometimes prayer lists can become heavy duties, accompanied by much guilt when the list fails to be prayed over. When you are following the Holy Spirit and not a list, there is no guilt. If a certain circumstance is not prayed over, you can trust that the issue is safely with Him. If He didn't think you needed to pray about it right then, who is there to condemn you? If Jesus only did what He saw the Father doing, and only said what He heard from the Father, how much more should we model that in our prayer life? What freedom! No more guilt for not remembering so-and-so and their big toe injury. No more guilt from well-meaning people saying: "How much more would you be praying if it was your child?" With the internet and television I could know about, and be requested to pray for, thousands of issues across the globe. What peace and rest to let the Lord sort them out and assign the prayers He wants to pray through me!

I encourage you; let the largest part of your prayer time be receiving your assignment from Him and then letting Him pray through you to fulfill it. Everything begins and ends with Him! Especially prayer!

What about intercession? What about people called to be intercessors? What about travail, identification, supplication? There are many books on intercession. Some are wonderful and some full of error. Many of these books break down the many ways the Spirit might intercede through a person attempting to describe and label them. For me, intercession is praying in the Spirit for someone else. Remember, we are to pray all kinds of prayer, always in the Spirit. Intercession is only one kind of prayer. If we are following Him, by looking and listening and then praying as He leads, then let's let Him worry about what kind of prayer He wants to use. We don't have to know anything except how to follow Him in prayer.

Tips for praying in the Spirit in groups

Many prayer-loving folks don't like to go to church prayer meetings because they feel they can't follow the Spirit there. It is more difficult, but let me tell you, when you can go together as a group where the Spirit leads, there is such a release of power! It is so precious, so powerful and effective! It is worth working out the kinks so we can enter into Spirit-led prayer together. A little bit of instruction goes a long way. Many people don't know how to follow the Spirit in their own prayer life. If we can instruct and mentor them in it, our corporate meetings will be so much more unified. Once you have a group of believers who know about and want to follow the Spirit in prayer, the following tips will help you flow together.

1. <u>Know when to share and when not to share</u>- If you have revelation from the Lord and the meeting is in a lull, share it. Even if it is seemingly just a piece and makes no sense, others may have a piece to fit with yours. Your sharing will encourage them to do likewise. As you flow with what the Spirit is saying/showing the group, you do not have to share everything you get. If the same theme has been shared with different examples, don't take up the prayer time with another, just to "prove" that the group is hearing from God. Only share what will move the group forward in praying or receiving what the Lord is saying.

2. <u>Don't pray like you are alone</u>- Many a prayer warrior causes the rest of the group to groan when they realize that "Sister Longwinded" is just getting started. When you are praying in a group, add what the Spirit is giving you, but be sensitive and know that He is likely not giving the entire job in prayer to you! Look for the Lord to move through the whole group. Be sensitive to the room at large and recognize when others begin to disengage. It could be because you are praying too long.

3. <u>Stay on subject</u>- When the unction in prayer is there for a group, everyone should be instructed not to change the subject of prayer lightly or too quickly. This cannot be stressed enough. If everyone will do this, it enables

the group to "pray through" on a subject and leave the meeting knowing that they have touched heaven and moved a mountain. When those who are just learning to follow the Spirit in prayer change the prayer topic before it should have been changed, it is up to the prayer leader or a more mature believer to "go back" and find the unction again.

4. <u>Be willing to go back</u>- Be willing, as the prayer leader or group member, to go back to the last time you felt the anointing or unction of the Holy Spirit. Learn to follow His lead as a group. It is easy for one person praying alone to miss it and have to go back and find the anointing. It is even easier for a group to miss it. However, when you find the unction together, there is nothing like it! One can put a thousand to flight, and two can put ten thousand to flight. No wonder the enemy tries to destroy unity in corporate prayer.

Chapter 7

What About Making Mistakes?

Few things have the potential to crush you like thinking you heard the Lord and then finding out you didn't. This book is about encouraging you to trust that if you ask, what comes to you is the answer. Have faith and receive. It really is that simple. I would be remiss, though, if I didn't look ahead of you on your journey of hearing, seeing, and dreaming and tell you that you will not always be perfect. 1 Corinthians 13:9 says that we know in part and we prophesy in part. When the words of the Lord flow through these earthen vessels of clay sometimes mistakes can be made. Sometimes it is in the hearing, like in my example in chapter one of thinking the Lord told me to go to Krogers. Sometimes we hear correctly, but put our own understanding on what we hear. Other times we just apply the rightly heard word in a wrong way.

Hopefully, by the time you have reached this, the last chapter of the book, you have already been hearing and seeing and receiving revelation from the Lord. You have, by this time, seen how hearing Him will change your own life and minister to those around you. It is my prayer that you have had success in branching out into new avenues of hearing from the Lord. This chapter is going to talk about what to do when you thought you heard the Lord and find out you didn't. What should you do? If you have come to rely on and act on what you are hearing, this could shake you to your core. My hope is that by accepting early on that it's okay to make a mistake, and in fact it is likely to happen, you will not be sidetracked or shipwrecked regarding your faith to receive in these ways.

I have had three major times when I thought I heard the Lord and later found out that I was mistaken in what I thought I heard. I want to talk about these times with you and help you glean something from my experience to help you on your journey. Before I talk about these three times, though, I think it is beneficial to mention that over decades of practicing and listening for revelation times of mishearing or misinterpreting what I have heard have been rare. What I have gained from these years of hearing is more than worth the price of facing the possibility of making a mistake. I do not want this chapter to cause any hindrance in trusting that what you hear is from the Lord. I don't want to cause anyone to be tempted to throw it all out because of a future chance of error.

The first time I thought I heard the Lord and didn't was shared in chapter one. I would just like to reiterate it and make a few points from the story here. I was new to the practice of hearing the voice of the Lord. I thought I heard the Lord tell me to go to Kroger's, which was the local grocery store. I thought that I would meet a man there wearing certain clothes and a red hat and that I was to pray for him because he was dying of cancer. I went to the store and there was no man there matching the description. I don't think I even saw a man in the store! I had come home feeling put out with the Lord. I was mad. I went back to the Lord and said, "What was that?!?" This was when He told me to get pen and paper and told me to write it down. He said, "Lesson number one, when I tell you to do something from inside you, it will *always* sound like you, not someone else's voice." That is when I realized that the "voice" I had heard in my thoughts sounded like my pastor and not me.

The first thing you should do when you make a mistake, or it seems as though you did not hear God, is go to Him! Go ask questions. Go straight to Him and not people. He will answer you. His answer that night satisfied me, and I was happy that I had learned a valuable lesson. Not only that, because He had said "number one", it led me to believe I was going to be schooled further. I was.

Hearing God's voice through others

The next time I thought I heard God and didn't was several years later. I was a missionary on the mission field in eastern Germany. I had many, many awesome testimonies of accurately hearing the Lord. Even getting to the field involved my husband and me hearing God about the same thing on the same day, separately from one another. He spoke and caused miraculous things to happen. My faith in my ability to hear God was at an all-time high. Then I had a dream. I knew this dream was important and that it was from God. However, I didn't have a clue what the dream meant. I had yet to learn about dreams or how to interpret them. My husband and I had a close friend who lived as a missionary in Italy at the time. This man had a gift for interpreting other people's dreams. First I took the dream to my husband. He began to tell me what he thought it meant. I didn't like his thoughts on it and said so. Then I went and sat down with a notebook and a pen and tried to get the meaning of it myself. I wrote a whole page full of things that I felt were from the Lord. I read them to my husband. He said that he did not think I heard rightly. So we sent the dream off to our friend via e-mail. When his reply came back you could have knocked me over with a feather. His interpretation was exactly the same as my husband's! Now I had a dilemma. I thought I had heard the Lord, a whole page worth of the Lord talking to me about my dream. Now I had to face that I had not heard the Lord. These two men heard the Lord.

This really threw me for a loop! The sound of the thoughts in my head sounded just like me, the way God's thoughts did. I thought it sounded just like the voice that told me to go to the mission field. It sounded just like the voice in my thoughts that I relied on time and time again. To say that I was upset is an understatement. I went to the Lord, asking what was up. I heard nothing. I began to complain before Him that if I didn't hear Him for the dream, maybe I never heard Him! Maybe I shouldn't be in Germany! He was silent for a while, while I vented all my feelings. I expected an answer from Him. I expected to hear, "Get your pencil, here is lesson number two." For days I heard nothing. Then He said very sternly to me, "Don't ever say you don't know if you heard me call you here or not again!" He went on to say, "You know you've heard me, and you know how to hear me." Just like that, I knew He was right. (duh!) Just like that my faith in hearing the Lord was restored. I still didn't have an explanation that was clear. I just realized, over time, that I didn't want my friend and my husband's interpretation, so I somehow "forced" a different answer. My interpretation stroked my ego, and the men's humbled me.

I didn't recognize the voice of the Lord coming through my husband. I rejected what was coming from him as not being from God, simply because I didn't like it. I never prayerfully considered it for even a moment. What folly! What arrogance!! Through this experience I learned to hear God's voice through others and not think that I have total and correct revelation on everything because I can hear Him. We are a body and need one another. We are to remain teachable and above all not think that our piece of the pie is the whole thing!! This lesson is very valuable and worth the price of the days that I was in turmoil and questioning everything I ever thought I heard. God can take even our mistakes and use them for our good. He is just that Awesome! Thank you, Lord!

Some advice that can keep you from having to go through what I did is never "force" it. Receiving is a passive word. There really isn't work involved, just connection. If you find yourself "trying" hard to hear something, just stop. Relax. Go into another topic with the Lord and just be with Him. Then, if you want to try asking Him about a particular thing again, go ahead. He may not want to talk about that right now for your own benefit. If you persist in performance mode you might end up with an answer that is from your own soul.

I just want to encourage you when you are thrown for a loop in the practice of receiving revelation from Him, always go back and "hear" about it from Him. The Holy Spirit is our teacher. The more revelation you receive from Him, the more important it is to know that as much as you receive, it is never the whole infallible revelation. Remain teachable, and allow for yourself to make a mistake without throwing away the rest of what you have heard.

The three W's

Normally in walking in the Spirit, you ask and believe that you receive what you have asked for. That includes hearing direction or information from God. Believing is done in rest. Sometimes in circumstances that evoke stress or high emotions, I find that I rely on the three W's: Worship, Willing, and Wait. The process these three words lead us through can keep us from making mistakes and lead us to a place of rest where we can simply receive the word of the Lord.

<u>Worship</u>- We must minimize the circumstance and ourselves and magnify God. If we will take our mind off the thing we need God to speak to us about and put our minds on Him, God becomes bigger than our problem in our sight. Worship and magnify God until you see the problem as insignificant in the light of who He is! Soak yourself in His goodness until your heart is at rest there. Then stay there and wait.

<u>Wait</u>- Don't be in a hurry. Be unwilling to go ahead without some leading from Him. Ask the Lord to confirm what you heard. Ask Him questions about what you have heard. Try to avoid asking Him questions with yes or no answers. Don't walk away with your thimble full of answers when He may have a bucket for you. Generally after worship and waiting you are now willing.

<u>Willing</u>- We must be like Jesus and be able to say not my will, but Yours be done in this situation. Jesus said in John 5:30 that He could trust His own judgment because the will of the Father was more important to Him than His own. You can be sure of what you hear from the Lord and obey Him from this place of surrender. You can be willing to take a risk.

The third time I thought I heard God and it seemed like I didn't was just a year before this writing. I had begun to have problems breathing through my nose. I had a large nose with a bump in the bridge that had always bothered me. When I went to the specialist, he said that I had a deviated septum that would require surgery to fix. I asked him if, while he was doing surgery, he could remove the bump. He said he could, and we scheduled the surgery. Before the surgery he ordered many scans and tests. One of these came back and indicated that I needed a much more invasive, severe sinus surgery. I ended up having four different kinds of sinus surgery and came through it fine. None of the terrible problems that could have occurred *during* surgery happened. Praise the Lord! However, the *results* of the surgery were disappointing.

I had had several words from the Lord about the surgery and about how I would be able to rest better, have more energy, and feel pretty when I went on a cruise that was planned for several months later. I was comforted by the words of the Lord and lay down for my surgery in faith.

When the bandages came off and the time that I was supposed to be able to go back into public came, I was appalled. I was very unhappy with the way it looked, and I still couldn't breathe out of it. I felt very, very ugly. I was so hurt and so disappointed! Not only was I unhappy with the results of the surgery, I was also unhappy because I felt like I couldn't have heard the Lord. I felt as though He let me down. I went back to my journal entries and re-read what He said. I know that sometimes we put our own understanding on what we think He said. I wanted to look at what I actually wrote down and not go by how I remembered or understood it. I read clearly the promises of resting better, more energy, and the promise of feeling pretty on my cruise. There it was in black and white. I had remembered the words correctly. I could not breathe better or get more rest, nor did I experience more energy. Also looking in the mirror was painful for me, because I focused on all that was wrong with how my nose looked. My circumstances seemed to fly in the face of what I had heard from the Lord. They were screaming in my soul, "Either you can't hear God or He lied to you!"

I had already had the previous two experiences with lots of years in between. How could I have missed God? I would need to have another surgery a year later to repair what was lacking in the first surgery. As my emotions began to settle down and people actually didn't even notice the changes in my nose, I reconciled that the word of the Lord to me was still true. It may not have come to pass when I thought it would, but I had renewed grace to believe for better rest and more energy, even if it required another step to do it. What about the cruise? There was a deadline. He said I would feel pretty. I've got to tell you that I thought there was no way that could happen. It was five months out. There were some small improvements over the five months in my nose, but the biggest change was in me.

I had some good advice from some awesome women of God. They told me to focus on what was good and beautiful in my features and not what I didn't like. I started to do it. The more I did the more at home with my new features I got. God also had many people compliment me and tell me I looked beautiful. More people noticed and commented on something about me being attractive in those five months than in the whole of my life before. Many of these people didn't even know I had had surgery, or they were meeting me for the first time. On top of that I know the Holy Spirit had many people who loved me praying for me. I don't really know all the ways in which He did it, but when I went on my cruise I did feel pretty! The word of the Lord that had a time limit was fulfilled. This amazes me. I did not try to make this happen, or do anything except try not to focus on the negative.

My conclusion is this: His word to me was true. I did hear Him. However, this word did not come to pass as I thought it would when I received it. My understanding was faulty, but His word was true. It has not fully come to pass yet. As of this writing I still have not had the second surgery. I know that the fulfillment of the word is coming. Don't be quick to think you did not hear the Lord. Go back to what He said. Go back to Him in prayer with questions. Wait for the word of the Lord with perseverance.

Offended with Him?

The lesson I want to encourage you with from my on-going testimony is this: Though I was offended, I didn't quit. How could I? I had a determination in my heart that He had the words of life! Where else was I supposed to go? Who else is there? When Jesus' disciples were offended at his sayings in John 6:65-68, Jesus asked them if they wanted to go away from Him because of it. They answered Him and said, "Lord, to whom shall we go? You have the words of eternal life."

If you have this same determination, this same realization that only His words are life, then you will finish the course. You will continue on this journey of hearing and receiving from Him until we see Him face to face. Holy Spirit will help you jump over every trial and obstacle as you move forward. Stay His pupil. Stay in a listening posture before Him. He is the Fountain of Life!

Matthew 11:6 (Amp.) *And blessed (happy, fortunate, and to be envied) is he who takes no offense at Me and finds no cause for stumbling in or through Me and is not hindered from seeing the Truth.*

Chapter 8

Testimonies

I am a firm believer in the power of our testimony. When someone hears a testimony, with the hearing comes faith to know that if God did it for someone else, He will do it for me. I have compiled some testimonies from people I know to encourage you on your journey of hearing and obeying God. Enjoy!

~~~~~~~~~~~~~~~~~~

We were cruising at 30,000 feet on our way to Colorado Springs. I was literally thinking about nothing when these words began to fall on the quietness of my mind. "When you see Linda tell her that I love her and that she and her children are in my hands and everything will be all right. The children will be fine." I knew it was the Holy Spirit asking me to give Linda this message.

When we arrived at our friend's home, I was informed that there was to be a cell group meeting on Wednesday night. Curious as to what the Lord was up to with Linda, I asked my friend if he had a lady named Linda in his group. He said "no". I asked if he knew a Linda. He said his secretary was named Linda and she would be at work on Thursday. I asked if I could meet with Linda before she went to work.

My wife and I asked her to have a seat and to listen to what I believed was a "word from the Lord". I told her I heard these words at 30,000 feet on the way to Colorado Springs. "When you see Linda, tell her that I love her and that she and her children are in my hands and everything will be all right. The children will be fine."

She immediately burst into tears! We asked her why she was crying. She said her husband had left her last week. Fear had gripped her about how she and her children were going to make it. We assured her the Lord was watching intently over her and the children.

We asked her if she was born again. She said she was Catholic. I asked if she had received Jesus into her life as her Lord and Savior. She said that she was Catholic. I told her I believed the Lord wanted a personal relationship with her. So we led her through the sinner's prayer and she was born again.

~Josh~

I had finished Bible School and had been working in a church office in the accounting department for several years. I had been praying about what God might want me to do for full time ministry. During these years after school, I had

110

remained very active in the worship department, doing a lot of singing and teaching on worship.

One morning as I was getting ready for work the thought suddenly came into my mind: "You will travel the country visiting churches singing, teaching on worship, and working with worship teams." It was as if the next years of my life were just that easily planned out.

At the time, I was not married. The first thought in my mind was, "I can't do this by myself." Even as I thought those words, I could almost see the Lord step back and look at me as though He was saying, "Did you just hear what you said?" I realized I was not alone. That He would be there every step of the way. I chose in that moment to take the first steps in embracing His plan for my immediate future.

I traveled the country for almost two years ministering in many churches. God was with me and I never felt alone. I was totally protected and provided for. I took the risk of obedience and discovered that He had already prepared the way.

~Tobi~

We were on a mission trip to Guadalajara, Mexico with a team from our School of Ministry. During the altar call, many were being touched by the Holy Spirit. I was listening intently to see if the Lord was through and we should end the service.

The Lord gave me a name, Rebecca. He said, "Call for Rebecca and tell her that I know her name." That was a very simple message. The prayer time was all but finished. The team and I were hungry as this was the second service of the day. I called for Rebecca and no one came. After a few minutes, I called for Rebecca again. Someone came to me and said that she had just left the building. I sent them to bring her back. Rebecca came to the front. I asked her if her name was Rebecca. She said yes. I told her the Lord gave me her name and that He had a message for her. He said to tell you that He knows your name. "Your name is Rebecca and I do know your name." Does that mean anything to you? Immediately, she burst into tears. I asked her why she was crying. She said she had enjoyed the service and decided to leave. She said she was going to go and commit suicide. I asked her why. She said that she had been struggling with her faith. She did not believe that God loved her and she did not believe God even knew her name.

This was a direct word of knowledge given to me by the Lord. When I hear words from the Lord they are like my own thoughts, but spontaneous, not analytical. They easily come as though God is speaking to me in the first person. They are often light, gentle, and are easily cut off by any exertion of self (own thoughts, will, etc.). They generally have an unusual content but are more wise, more loving, and motive-oriented than my own thoughts.

~Josh~

As most Christians who are newly filled with the Holy Spirit, I found that my Bible really came alive to me. I got very attached to my Bible because it was full of notations of things God was speaking to me while reading it. One day, I could not find it. I pondered all the scenarios of where it could be and where I could have lost it. On the verge of tears because of my attachment to it, I said, "Oh, Jesus, I really love that Bible and I can't find it anywhere." I heard the Lord reply; "Go dust." "Go dust?" I asked. "Lord, are you not concerned? I lost my Bible with all the things You have spoken to me written in it." His response was the same, "Go dust." Deciding to be obedient, I opened my linen closet to get a dust cloth. There it was; my beloved bible. Apparently, I had it in my hand when putting away laundry and laid it down to stack linens. I learned an important lesson that day. Sometimes His instructions do not seem logical to us, but they are perfectly logical to Him.

~Gracie~

Many years ago when we lived in our first home, I had a dream early on a Sunday morning. In the dream, I saw people that had tried to lure me into the cult called The Way some years earlier. They looked very friendly, but were full of lies and sin. At the end of the dream, I saw myself rising up with boldness and exposing their lies with Scripture, then challenging them to repent and come out of this bondage. I woke up and shared this strange dream with my wife.

After church that day, there was a young couple that was coming by to pick up a puppy that we were selling them. As they walked through our home and saw Scriptures, they commented that they were Christians too. I rejoiced and remarked on the goodness of God, but I kept getting a "dead wood" response from them. There was no spiritual affinity. It seemed odd. I asked what church they were part of and they responded, "We meet in small groups in homes."

I remember the next moment so clearly, though it was more than 20 years ago. As I walked up my stairs to get something, like a bolt of lightning, God brought the dream back to me and let me know they were from this cult. I halted in mid-stairs, turned to them sitting in my living room and said, "God spoke to me about you in a dream last night. You are from the The Way group, and you know such and such people (I had seen them in the dream). You meet in small groups called twigs." At first they were rattled, but elated. Everything was true! Then, I came down and said, "He showed me what to tell you." I revealed the fallacy in the cult, exposed its dangers and encouraged them to get out of it. I said that I would meet with any leader and share why they are wrong.

We never met again, but talked by phone and they appreciated all I said. They were never able to organize an encounter with their leaders. I assume they eventually got out, but never heard the results. God spoke and guided by a dream.

~John~

At the end of our services at church, the prayer team is responsible for praying with people at the altar. When praying for the needs of others I am more comfortable preparing ahead of time, then seeking God's heart for them and scheduling a time to minister. "On the spot" ministry is more challenging for me and I am less likely to sense that I have correctly heard from God in those situations. So one Sunday morning before the altar call, I asked Father, "What kind of issues are the people that I am going to pray with today going to have?" I did not see or hear anything; I just had a knowing in my heart what the issues would be and also knew the general direction the prayer would take. It happened that I prayed with two women that morning both of whom had the particular issue I had perceived. It was amazing to see the change of countenance on their faces as the prayers progressed. I had a greater confidence or faith as I was praying because I was certain of what I had perceived ahead of time.

~Gracie~

I was working in the business world and doing ministry on weekends and evenings for many years. At the same time, we were raising a family with four children. The scheduling pressure of life was so intense. I felt I would burst! Though my life was marked with miracles, I started crying out to God - asking Him to talk to me about what to do. But, I heard nothing. I felt I could not hear from God right. I felt there must be something wrong with me.

I attended a men's retreat that year, 1989, and was impressed to fast half the meals and pray. On the last night, I was standing during a worship time saying, "Oh God, why can't I hear from you? Please open my ears. Speak! Do something!" Suddenly, God began to speak in my head in sentences! He first rebuked me. "You were not able to hear because your unbelief was in the way. Doesn't my Word say, "My sheep hear my voice?" I instantly repented. Then, He poured out to me both challenges and keys that would mark my life ministry, such as; walking through battering wind and waves, while walking on water.

A minute later, a brother came from the back of the room. He said, "I just had a vision of you walking on water and being battered by winds and waves, but you were making it." I knew I had clearly heard from God to go into full-time ministry. It took two years for God to work us through the timing, speak to my wife, and open the right doors. It all worked out. I learned that the principles of Hebrews 11:6 are still in effect. "But without faith it is impossible to please Him, for he who comes to God must believe that He is, and He is a rewarder of those who diligently seek Him".

~John~

In 1992, I was in prayer in my bedroom when I heard a voice deep inside of me say, "Manila." At that moment, I could not even remember where it was. I thought "Manila. Where is that? Indonesia - India - Philippines?" The latter was right. That morning when I went to my office, there was a document from an organization in the Philippines. I knew that I was to go. I continued to pray, and the pieces fell into place. Obedience is so critical.

I organized a trip and three people accompanied me, later that year. When I arrived in Manila, it was sheer confusion. People grabbed our luggage, taxis bullied us and the air was heavy - welcome to Manila. We had directions to go to a certain hotel and wait. And we waited and waited and waited for hours. But, I knew God sent us and He would work it out. At one point, I was standing in the lobby about 100 feet from the check-in counter and I heard in my head, "Walk to the counter now." I walked to one point of this expansive counter, and as I approached, a bellhop answered the phone and repeated, "You want to speak to John so and so." I said, "I am right here" and he handed me the phone. It was my contact.

On that trip, I saw some of the greatest miracles of God as we followed the voice of the Lord in ministry. It was always a word in our hearts, and then confirming circumstances. One day, God told me to preach on the man that picked up his bed when Jesus forgave and healed him. As I peeked outside my sleeping tent, a man walked by carrying his bed! Well, I preached with fire that night, and repentance and healing broke out everywhere. We saw a great revival that went on for about 3 months after we left. Every one of those who were with me on the trip obeyed the call to world missions and ministry.

In Acts 8, we see Philip on the go ministering everywhere. He just flowed and obeyed. In the second half, it says an angel spoke to him, then the Spirit spoke to him, and then he just took advantage of the circumstances he saw and spoke to the charioteer reading the Scripture. After leading him to Christ and baptizing him, the Spirit took him elsewhere. God will engineer everything and you will not miss the cues, as long as you are expectant and obedient.

~John~

My husband and I were foster parents for a period of about 8 years. One Saturday night, I had a dream. In the dream, my husband and I, as well as our children, I were driving in our vehicle on a mountainous road with many curves. We stopped near the top and someone put a baby boy in our car. The entire family was joyful about the baby boy. We continued driving along the road and noticed we could not see well around the curves.

That Sunday morning, someone at church said to me "I put some baby clothes in your car." When I got home, I saw that they all were baby boy clothes! These were not regular sizes, but very small size clothes, the kind a premature baby might need. I became expectant that we were going to receive a boy foster baby soon.

A short time later, we were asked to be foster parents to a baby boy. He was very small for his age. He hadn't been fed well and had trouble eating. We were joyous to have this sweet and beautiful baby boy (who I will call Caleb) in our home! We cared for him and loved him as our own. He stayed with us several months and we were told we might be able to adopt him. We were overjoyed! Then we were told he would be going back to his biological family. This was the curving road part of the dream, as we were told that we could and couldn't adopt Caleb by turns.

Finally, he did return to his biological family and I was heartbroken. I asked the Lord to speak to me out of the Scriptures to help me understand what His purpose for this baby and for us exactly was. I felt like the Lord gave me these two verses: Jeremiah 28:3 and 11. Both verses have the phrase "within two years". At the time, I wondered what that could mean. I wondered if this meant Caleb would return to our home within two years. As time went on I found myself grieving for little Caleb and missing him badly. I had even become a little bitter.

One morning my phone rang and it was a representative of the courts who said, "Caleb may have to be removed from his biological mom again and if so, he will assuredly be adoptable." She wanted to let us know so we could petition the court for him. I thanked her and hung up the phone. I went to my Bible and opened it up. It fell open at Jeremiah 28 and my eyes were drawn to verses 3 and 11 because I had circled them with a pen. I remembered these were the two verses God gave me when Caleb left our home. I calculated and realized it had been just under two years since the day little Caleb left our home!

I prayed and asked God what did this mean? I heard His voice inside me say "What do you want? Do you want Caleb to come back to your family?" At that point, I realized I had been focused on my feelings and not what was God's perfect will for Caleb. I repented and asked God what He wanted for Caleb. He told me His will was for Caleb to be loved and cared for properly by his birth mother and father. I aligned with God and prayed for this to happen and spoke blessing over Caleb's parents. I committed to pray for him over his growing up years. My broken heart healed and I did not retain the bitterness I had been feeling. I was free to become a prayer warrior for this little boy instead of nurse my feelings of loss and disappointment. I am honored to partner with our

God who loved and poured out His blessing on this little child.

~Georgette~

In late 2008 my video business had gone under and the last of my life's savings was gone (almost $200,000). I woke up in the middle of the night and was feeling my way in the pitch darkness to the kitchen for a drink, when I saw in a vision. I saw a large pickle jar before me filled with money. Then it tipped over and all the money spilled right out. It then came back upright again and it was full of money. Then, I heard a voice in my mind say, "Try me, spend it and see if I don't fill it again." I was in a pretty dark place in my life back then, and it took a couple of years for me to even share this, but we are now living in this place of His full provision!

~Bill~

I hear the Lord often through impressions or a sudden knowing that wasn't there a moment before. One time, my wife and I were shopping for a car. We really needed a car, but weren't sure if the financial commitment was a smart decision at that point in our lives. Our need for a car outweighed our reservations, and we found ourselves sitting across the desk from the salesman to negotiate a price for the car. We made an offer and the salesman left the office to print out some paperwork. I suddenly had an overwhelming impression that I needed to call my mom. I turned to my wife and said, "I have to call mom." My wife was not appreciative of the timing. "You have to call her, right now? He's going to be back any minute!" The impression was still so strong, and so I went outside to call my mom. When I reached her, she said that she had been trying to call me for three days. She had apparently left messages with our children that we never received. She had been trying to reach me to tell me that she was going to give me her car instead of sell it. In shock, I hung up the phone and returned to my wife. The car we were going to buy was a little compact sedan, and the car my mom was giving us was a very nicely kept, used Lincoln Continental. I told my wife what happened. Then the salesman returned and I told him that while he was away from the desk someone gave us a Lincoln Continental and that we did not want to buy a car from him anymore. I think it's safe to say that exact situation had never happened to him before. We thank God that He speaks through impressions and that He kept us from buying something that was inferior to what He was trying to give us for free!

~Doug~

I had fallen in love with a beautiful Christian girl. She was considerably younger than me. My parents were not originally in favor of the match. During dinner one night with my parents, they confronted me about Suzi, her age and her strange religion. (Christian Jew) My heart was broken. I had been saved 8 months earlier and was enjoying a good relationship with my folks after a decade of rebellion and drug abuse. Now I was being rejected by them for righteousness sake. I went into my room after dinner and started crying out to God in my frustration. I heard the words, "I never said it wouldn't hurt." Immediately after that, this time in my thoughts, came the words, "Trust in the Lord." Then I heard, in my thoughts again, "Trust in the Lord with all your heart." Then again, "Trust in the Lord with all your heart and lean not on your own understanding. In all thy ways acknowledge Him and He will direct your paths. "Wow! Where did that come from?" I thought to myself. It must be Scripture. When I called Suzi to tell her, she asked her roommate if she was familiar with what I heard. She told us it was Proverbs 3:5-6.

~Bill~

Our church was holding a Women's Conference and I decided to go on Friday night. In the middle of worship, one of the speakers took the microphone and said, "I have a word for someone. It is very specific and if this is you, don't hesitate or come up to me later, but stand up right away. Today, you sat in your car having lunch. When you went to eat that chocolate candy bar, it was a big melted mess. You ate half of it but decided it was too messy. So you put it back in the bag, thinking to yourself, 'I'll put it in the freezer when I get home and eat it later.' Who is it?" Well! That was so amazingly me, even down to the thoughts I had. You can believe that I stood up quick! Then she proceeded to speak prophetically over me. Women all over the room were nodding their heads and agreeing with things she said. I'm glad it was recorded! I was so overwhelmed with the realization that the Lord sees and knows my every thought, and really wanted to speak to me that I hardly heard what she said! I do remember that she said "Mother of Israel, mother of Israel, mother of Israel, mother of Israel!" This was confirmation of what the Lord had been saying to me and He has recently begun explaining what that means and placing me to fulfill that role.

~Francine~

I was in southern California visiting family, when I inadvertently offended my sister. After some time, she proceeded to tell me exactly what she thought of me, in no uncertain or pleasant terms. Very upset, I went outside and sat on a ledge in her backyard. As I sat there, on that typically beautiful, sunny California day, it suddenly began to rain. No torrential downpour, just a light, lovely sprinkle from a clear blue sky. Then a hummingbird came and hovered right in front of me. I could see it looking at me. If I had reached out, I could have touched it. I knew that the Lord was telling me that He was with me, comforting me as only He could do. The Lord often speaks to me through nature. I find it wonderful that He causes even the creatures to do His bidding, so that I can know of His love for me!

~Francine~

About thirty years ago, my husband felt that God was calling him to quit his job and move to another state to go to school. We had three growing boys and I was a stay at home mom. Needless to say, my main concern was how in the world we were going to feed our family if we made such a radical change in our lives. Having grown up with meager means myself, trusting God for provision was a huge challenge for me and I was not eager to leave the 'security' of a steady income and put my own children through some of the same challenges I had growing up. I was in constant conversation with God about this.

One day I noticed a bird sitting on our back fence and I very gingerly walked over to approach it. To my surprise the bird not only allowed me to get close, but I actually picked it up and held it in my hand. This 'circumstance' got my attention and immediately the Scripture about God taking care of the birds of the air came to me. In that Scripture, I knew that Jesus had posed a rhetorical question about our being of more value than the birds. I remember feeling so special that day because just how many wild birds have most people held in their hand? However, my heart was not yet sure that I could trust God for provision. Several days later, I was driving by a fast food restaurant when I noticed a bird fly down to the ground and pick up a piece of a hamburger someone had thrown on the ground. Then I remembered how God commanded the birds to bring bread and meat to Elijah by the Brook Cherith.

Through these two circumstances, I felt He was saying to me that if He had to have the birds bring us food, He would and that I could trust Him to take care of us. There were many challenges through those years and trusting God was not easy, but the stories of His miraculous provision for us during that time period are too numerous to tell.

Some years after those experiences when we were in a more financially secure position, I actually began to miss the miraculous hand of God. I was quick to tell God that I did not want to go back to being financially needy again, however, I asked Him one night as I was leaving church if we were back in that needy situation again in the current city in which we were living, were there people here that would listen to Him to meet our needs. I heard no immediate answer and went on to the grocery store on my way home. To my surprise, the lady in the grocery line behind me said to the clerk, "I would like to pay for this lady's groceries." I greatly protested, knowing that in my heart it was God's way of answering my question to Him. She insisted and when we got outside the store, she said to me; "When you were going out of church tonight, I saw you and God told me to follow you wherever you went and pay for whatever you bought. Do you want to go fill up your car with gas?" Of course, I thanked her for obeying God and told her that it meant more to me than I could explain, but I did not want her to buy gas for me. I did remember seeing that lady at another church I had visited, but I had never seen her at our church. And to my knowledge, I have not seen her since that night. Even now I weep when I think of how good He is and that He is willing to prove Himself to us.

~Gracie~

I was praying for a couple once that had been married for several years. As soon as I laid hands on her, I *knew* she was pregnant. It turned out that they had been trying to get pregnant and she didn't even know yet that she was!

~Francine~

I was desperate to know God's will regarding Suzi and I. I was out of town in a hotel room in Denver, Co. and I had just heard a word on the radio about sitting before the Lord in silence to hear His voice. I told God that I needed to know if Suzi and I were to be together, because I was now falling in love with her and things were serious. I slid off the end of the bed and took a deep breath and before I could let it all out, the room opened up into what seemed to me was deep space. In my frame of vision all I could see was a myriad of stars. I looked down and saw a crystal door frame and door that was opened. Then Suzi and I appeared standing in the doorway facing each other. My view was from the right and above behind me where I could see Suzi's face and her expression was one of adoration and love. We then turned to face the doorway, joined arms and walked through the door. We turned back to face each other and the doorway went up out of sight and then the vision disappeared as quickly as it began. I later had the interpretation that our relationship was made in heaven. The stars were the angels as witnesses. The doorway was Jesus and we walked through Him together as one.

~Bill~

During prayer ministry, I will often see a path in front of the person I am praying for. The details vary widely, according to each individual. Sometimes it is wide, sometimes narrow. Sometimes the path splits and the Lord will say "You choose!" Sometimes the path will come with a warning... "Stay on it. If you step off, repent quickly and get back on!" Sometimes the path zigzags, and I know that the Lord is saying that changes are coming, or things are not going to be what you were expecting. The Lord is communicating with me visually to help me minister to their needs.

~Francine~

When I was 24 and looking for God, I came to point in my life where I realized I could not live a righteous life. I had just been through drug and alcohol treatment and had had a relapse which sent me into a spiral of self-loathing, shame and guilt. I cried out to God asking why he created me! Why was I on this earth! I literally cried myself to sleep. At around 4 AM, I was startled awake by a voice that said, "Minister." It really freaked me out and as I was trying to figure out what was going on, a physical feeling like a blanket came over me and enveloped me in a deep peace. When I closed my eyes, I saw MINISTER written across my mind's eye.

~Bill~

Once I was in a small group meeting with like-minded friends and believers. We were seated in a circle around the room. As we were singing and worshipping, I saw "in the Spirit" or with my "mind's eye", Jesus walking into the room. He stood in the middle of the circle.

I was always looking "in the Spirit" to see when I could do the things I saw Jesus doing. He got down on His knees in front of an older woman. He looked up at her and then laid His hands on her feet. He began to cry. The drops of His tears were hot and large. They seemed to flow from His eyes like a small stream onto her feet. I could feel His heart reaching out to her.

Suddenly, He stood up and looked right into my eyes. I asked Him, "What did all this mean?" I then saw myself doing exactly what Jesus had done. It was like I saw myself getting up, going over and laying hands on her feet. I began to cry. Once again, I asked, "What do you want me to do?" He said, "Do the things I just did. Tell her how much I love her. Tell her that I am bringing her husband home to be with me very soon."

I was doing ok with this until I was asked to pronounce a death sentence on her husband! I actually questioned the purpose for doing such a thing to this lady. What if I was wrong? At this point in time I had to decide to believe what I was seeing in the Spirit and be obedient to the vision I had just witnessed.

When the singing ended, I told the group what I had just seen in the Spirit except the part about telling her that Jesus was soon going to bring her husband home to Him. I asked the lady if I could come over and lay hands on her feet and pray for her. She said, "Yes."

I got down on my knees in front of her. I laid my hands on her feet. Suddenly, I began to openly weep and cry for her. I am not usually one to cry. The tears from my eyes felt like a hot stream pouring from my eyes on her feet until they were completely wet. The tears were uncontrollable. I was overwhelmed with the presence and love of God.

Then, I heard the Lord say to me, "Tell her." I wrestled with myself for a moment or two, trying to understand what the consequences would be if I was wrong in telling her that her husband was being called home to be with Jesus.

I set aside my fears, called up all the courage I could, and I said, "I have a message for you from Jesus. May I share with you what I think He told me to tell you?" She said, "Yes". "Jesus loves you very much. He has heard your heart's cry and he will soon take your husband home to be with him." She began to cry as did almost everyone in the circle. I could tell this struck a nerve among all of them.

I asked her why she was crying. She said, "My husband is old and has been in a vegetative state and comma for some time. We have been asking the Lord to heal him or take him home to heaven."

I was never as relieved and elated as I was when I heard those words. This small group had been praying for the Lord to intervene for some time, and now He was answering.

This was a Friday night. Her husband went home to be with Jesus on Monday. The Lord truly wanted to bless that group by revealing His intentions and informing them of what He was about to do.

Habakkuk 2:1 (NIV) *"I will stand at my watch…I will look to SEE what He will say to me…"*

We must realize that we can have encounters with Jesus, with God, and with angels in visions within our minds. These are actual spiritual encounters.

In John 5:19-20, Jesus gave them this answer: *"I tell you the truth, the Son can do nothing by Himself; He can do only what He sees His Father doing, because whatever the Father does the Son also does. For the Father loves the Son and shows Him all He does."*

~Josh~

In my days as a banker, I was sent oversees to take a look at the Global Trust operation within a few weeks of my hire by Chase Manhattan Bank in NYC. I was asked to just observe and report back what my general impression was.

God directed me to a multi-million dollar financial issue. I returned to the states and asked God to help me bring a solution to the problem and not just report the problem. God gave me a dream that I communicated to my new boss. It made little sense to me (I was new in the trust business) but, this began a 5 year project that ultimately made the bank money instead of a well over 100 million dollar potential loss.

~Gary~

My husband worked a variety of jobs, but always sensed that they were not permanent and that God had something different for him. This became a matter of constant prayer. One afternoon, I took a nap and had a dream in which I was talking to God about my husband's need. In the dream, the then governor of our state walked in and said that he had a job for my husband. I knew what the job was in the dream and got excited because I felt this was a good fit for him. When I awoke, I could not remember what the job was, but I did remember what our then governor said. That governor served seven more years and seemingly no "good fit" job happened for my husband. It was nineteen years after the dream that the manifestation came. The man who was governor of our state when I had the dream ran for governor again and won. It was during this term that my husband became a school administrator. This was the job that has been the best fit for him. He was like a pastor to them as well as an administrator. It has been a very rewarding experience for him. Although he is retired, the school system stills calls him back in to help with difficult situations. I know in my heart, that this was the job God was showing me in the dream. The word of the Lord does not lie. We sometimes must wait for it, but God is faithful. Although the years of waiting for God's answer were challenging to our faith, it is easy to look back now and see that the years between the dream and the manifestation were years of preparation for what God had for us.

~Gracie~

I hope you are as encouraged by these testimonies as I am. They are a great testimony to our need to hear from Him in every facet of our lives. When trouble comes, blessed is the child of God who has been taught to know and follow the voice of God.

Appendix A

These are a collection of some meditations on the times that Scripture says Jesus blood was shed. A friend of mine spent some time meditating on these times in Scripture with the Holy Spirit. She allowed me to include them here, so you could see the rich depth of intimacy with the Lord that comes from this kind of meditation. I hope they bless you as much as they did me.

MEDITATIONS ON THE BLOOD OF JESUS
By Gracie Denton

In The Garden

(Between 8:45 and 9:25 am on August 30, 2010)

I began to picture Jesus in the Garden of Gethsemane on His knees praying to the Father. I was sitting on my knees watching Him. His hands were on the ground supporting the weight of His body and the weight of the stress that was on Him. His muscles bulged and the veins in His arms were popped up. Sweat was pouring down His arms. As I focused on His face, I could see in His eyes a mixture of love and sadness. I could see the sweat drops on His brow as they turned to blood. I wanted to reach out and touch the blood.

He managed to raise one hand and extend it to me in invitation to come to Him. It amazed me that He had the capacity to see me and focus on me in the midst of all the pain and suffering He was enduring. I was reminded that it was for me that He went through all that He went through. As I came closer, I found myself encased under His chest. I thought for sure that I would feel the weight of all that was crushing Him. Instead, all of the pain and all of the weight was on Him and I was totally protected from feeling and sensing ANY of it. Then I found myself in a place that was full of light. Before I could ask where I was, I knew that I was in Jesus' heart. There was no darkness at all in His heart - not one iota of darkness. I remembered the Scripture, "In Him was no darkness at all." There was a realization that although the stress on Jesus' body and His soul in the garden came close to killing Him (He said, "My soul is exceedingly sorrowful even unto death."), none of it could touch His Spirit. His Spirit never became defiled and that is where He was hiding me. Then I heard Holy Spirit say, "This is the same spirit that burst forth from Jesus on the Mount of Transfiguration." Then I wondered if Jesus was having a 'flashback' to the mount and remembering the things that Moses and Elijah said to Him there to prepare Him for His sufferings. Did He draw strength from that memory? Then Holy Spirit said, "And this is the same Spirit that raised Him from the dead when this was all over." Wow, to think that I was encased in the Spirit of the living Christ, being protected from all that He was bearing for me. Then I came out of that

136

place and just looked at Him in awe. I eased over to Him, not in fear, but with a worshipful heart and kissed Him on the forehead to just say thank You, thank You, thank You for this precious gift of Your blood that You are giving to me. As I backed away I could sense the sweetness, the power, and the love that was in the blood filling me. Then I saw angels coming to minister to Him. As they came, the first thing they did was bow in worship before Him. Then they surrounded Him, touching Him, encasing Him much like I was being encased by Him and encouraging Him. All I could do in my spirit was weep with joy at what He was accomplishing for me - taking all my stress, making it possible for me to cast all my care upon Him, bringing me to a higher trust level. Then the old hymn, 'Jesus paid it all' came to me and I began singing it in worship to Him.

A new understanding of the Scripture, "They overcame him by the blood of the lamb and the word of their testimony." came to me. What is the word of their testimony? The word of their testimony is what the blood can do!

His Marred Face

> Isaiah 52:14 *"Just as many were astonished at you, My people, so His appearance was marred more than any man, and His form more than the sons of men."*

> Matt 26: 67-68 *"Then they spat in His face and beat Him with their fists; and others slapped Him, and*

said, 'Prophesy to us, You Christ; who is the one who
hit You?'"

I placed myself in the scene of Jesus before the soldiers where
He was beaten beyond recognition. As soon as the first slap
came across Jesus' face, it was as though an infinitely long
strip of film appeared before Him. It was somehow
suspended in space and ran from the beginning of time on
into the future. On it were scenes depicting men slandering
and judging one another. There were scenes from the
holocaust, of innocent Jews and Christians being rejected just
because of who they were. Other scenes were of parents
abusing children, husbands abusing wives. It seemed as
though every form of one human being rejecting another
appeared before Him. With each scene on the filmstrip and
with each fist on His face, He said, "Yes, I'll bear that one.
Yes, I'll take that one. Yes, put that one on me." It seemed as
if the abuse to His head and face would not stop. His
tormentors were insatiable. As His face swelled and the
blood began to flow, I cried out, "Oh, Jesus, make them stop.
Make them stop. You do not deserve this." It was then that
He allowed me to get a closer look at the strip of film. There
on the film strip were my personal sins of rejection, scenes of
both those who had demeaned and rejected me, as well as
those whom I had demeaned and rejected. I looked at Jesus'
face and one corner of His bloody swollen lip managed a
smile. His eyes, oh His eyes, said, "But it was for you. If I
don't do this, you cannot know Me and you cannot be healed
of your rejection." My heart acquiesced in homage and

138

silence before Him. Tears of gratitude began to flow-gratitude for His forgiveness of my sins of rejection and gratitude for giving me the willingness and grace to forgive those who had rejected me.

Then before me appeared a painting with multiple colors of reds, blues, greens and yellows. It was not a particularly impressive painting, but the artist who painted it was very proud of it. I saw men go up to it and scratch it. One took a nail and made a zigzag scratch on it, some threw paint on it. Others just made fun of it and laughingly asked, "What's so special about that painting?", as if they could see no value in it. The countenance of the artist fell as He dropped His head in sorrow at what was being done to the painting. The men just continued to mock. I had a knowing that if one drop of Jesus' blood touched the painting, it would be returned to its original image. The men who had marred it would stop and stand in silence. The heart of the Artist would smile. "What am I seeing, Lord, what does this mean?" I asked. Understanding began to come to me. Each of our lives is a unique portrait made in the image of God. When men reject and slander each other, they slander the image of God. The enemy throws "paint" on us in an attempt to create a different image. Sometimes that image gets marred beyond recognition even as the face of Jesus did. God's heart is sad. Jesus bore disfigurement in His face so that we might be restored to God's original design and that we might be free to stop judging and rejecting one another. God's heart can smile again.

The Piercing of His Hands

As I began to meditate on the nails being hammered through Jesus' hands, I could see the grimace of pain on His face. My heart gasped and I was unable to look upon the sight. I wondered if He remembered when His hands were used in the beginning to form the dust of the earth into the very vessel that was now piercing his hands. Oh, the love that would say, "Yes, take these hands that have formed you, that have been offered in service to you, I surrender them to you to do with as you will." All the destruction for which man could use his hands was being paid for when His Holy Hands were pierced through. "Whatever you put your hands to will prosper." This seemed to be the promise flowing from His heart as He endured the pain. Redeemed hands would now do the work of His hands. I could see myself touching my grandchildren and it was as though Jesus Himself was touching them. As I saw myself touching my husband, my children, my friends and people I did not even know, The Lord said, "When you touch them, I will touch them. Your touch has now become My touch."

Then I saw some of the same hands that had hammered the nails through His hands throw down their hammers, fall on their knees and begin to worship Him. I looked at Jesus to see His reaction and I could hear His heart answer, "Even these hands that have pierced the holiest of all hands can be redeemed and can become hands of blessing." The wrath of God over the evil deeds of men's hands had been satisfied.

Psalm 138:8 *"The Lord will accomplish what concerns me; Your loving kindness, O Lord, is everlasting; Do not forsake the works of Your hands."*

Psalm 57:2 *"I will cry to God Most High, to God who accomplishes all things for me."*

Presentation of the Blood

As I returned to the place of prayer and meditation on the blood of Jesus, I sensed the Lord calling me back to the place in His heart that I had entered into when meditating on the blood that was shed in the garden. As I entered His spirit there, suddenly I could see Jesus in the tomb. Then His Spirit literally burst out of Him and He was resurrected. I then saw Him stand before the Father with a vessel in His hands. He said, "Father, here is the blood." The angels gathered around and looked in the bowl. They began to excitedly announce all over heaven, "It's the blood. It's the blood. It's here! He did it! It's here! He did it!" There was excitement everywhere because the blood was being presented. I thought of the joy when the Ark of the Covenant was returned to God's people. The Father looked at the blood, then up at Jesus and said, "You are my beloved Son. I am well pleased with you." Jesus then began to take the blood and sprinkle it over the mercy seat and onto a book. Then I saw Him sprinkle it into the very atmosphere of Heaven. I saw Him sprinkle it on the ground and somehow it became foundations to houses that would be prepared for the saints. All of heaven was somehow changed when the blood was sprinkled. Everything became more alive and heaven was taken to a whole new level.

Hebrews 12:22-24 *"But you have come to Mt. Zion and to the city of the living God, the heavenly Jerusalem and to myriads of angels, to the assembly and church of the firstborn who are enrolled in heaven, and to God, the judge of all, and to the spirits of the righteous made perfect, and to Jesus the mediator of a new covenant, and to the sprinkled blood which speaks of better things..."*

Hebrews 9:19 *"Moses took the blood of goats and calves and sprinkled the book itself and all the people."*

Hebrews 9:24 *"For Christ did not enter a holy place made with hands, a mere copy of the true one, but into heaven itself, now to appear in the presence of God for us."*

Ephesians 2:6 *"But God ...raised us up with Him, and seated us with Him in the heavenly places in Christ Jesus ..."*

The information in this book was designed to be taught in seminar format or as an in-depth 6-week course with ample time for instruction and practicing of the exercises. However, Kathy has developed a shorter format for a single visit to a church or small group. If you would like to have Kathy conduct a seminar for your church or group please contact her at **kathyatcore@gmail.com**. If you are interested in hosting a 6-week course, there is also a workbook with study questions available as an additional resource.

CPSIA information can be obtained at www.ICGtesting.com
Printed in the USA
BVOW05s0024200314

348216BV00007B/78/P